A FOURTH WORLD

An Anthropological-Ecological Look at the Twenty-First Century

Bernard J. James

University Press of America, Inc.
Lanham • New York • Oxford

Copyright © 1997 by
University Press of America,® Inc.
4720 Boston Way
Lanham, Maryland 20706

12 Hid's Copse Rd.
Cummor Hill, Oxford OX2 9JJ

Library of Congress Cataloging-in-Publication Data

James, Bernard J.
A fourth world : an anthropological-ecological look at the twenty-first
century / Bernard J. James.
p.   cm.
l. Civilization, Modern. 2. Twenty-first century--Forecasts. 3.
Human ecology. 4. Anthropology--Philosophy.   I. Title.
CB358.J346 1997   909.83--dc21   97-8867 CIP

ISBN 0-7618-0762-4 (cloth: alk. ppr.)
ISBN 0-7618-0763-2 (pbk: alk. ppr.)

Dedicated to Kathleen

Contents

Preface

Because a good deal of this book concerns historical events in sequence over several centuries, for the reader's convenience I have included many citations by name and date in the body of the manuscript rather than as a series of numbered references chapter by chapter in the bibliography at the end of the volume.

About the Author

Bernard J. James, Ph.D., is Professor Emeritus of Anthropology at the University of Wisconsin-Milwaukee, where he served as Chairman of the Department of Anthropology and Director of the Center for Advanced Study in Organization Science, with programs in Madison and Milwaukee. Prior to coming to the University of Wisconsin, he was Lecturer in Political Science at The University of Chicago and Director of its Center for Programs in Government Administration and its Institute for Psychiatric Administration. He is author of *The Death of Progress*, a book about the sociology of ideas, numerous professional papers and two novels, *Greenhouse* and *Milwaukee the Beautiful*. He resides in Bayside, Wisconsin with his wife, Kathleen Ryan.

Chapter 1

Concerning Sin and Shadow

Early in the morning of February 12, 1994, two men pulled a van up outside Norway's National Gallery in Oslo, broke a window, entered the museum, and stole Edvard Munch's famous painting called *The Scream*. It was later recovered. The theft itself was not all that surprising. Security at the museum was poor, and the painting was renowned as an emblem of our age, and worth a lot of money. So from one point of view, stealing the painting made good sense, even though it was recovered by the museum after a million dollars had been offered the burglars in a sting operation. I believe the thieves went to jail. So from another point of view, the theft did not make much sense.

Painted in 1893, *The Scream* seems to foretell what the twentieth century held in store for mankind. Its central figure, hollow-cheeked, skull-like, its hands pressed to its ears as if to shut out some terrible truth, or to quench the madness within its own imagination of the future, runs along a jetty toward us, crying out its terror.

I do not know what Munch really was up to when he painted *The Scream*. Some say it is an existentialist statement. Others say Munch simply enjoyed probing human emotions with his palette and brushes. But certainly one is safe in saying that this painting is not right for the walls of the average Optimists Club, or even the Rotary. And despite our natural desire to slip loose from pessimism, even though it is very often a useful predictor in life, it does at times seem that modern mankind is careening, like the creature in Munch's painting, toward some horrifying abyss.

What Munch's creature may have seen is the end of the modernist world arriving across the planet in the next century, not in some terrible, sudden Armageddon, but in a thousand small, famine-ridden, disease-infested struggles for space and resources on an ecologically wasted planet. The present outburst of treacherous localisms, secessions, tribalisms and ethnic struggles that now scourge the world seem to be early signs of this likely fate, a unique fate, certainly on a global scale.

Seeing a positive side to this great, grim tableau is a daunting challenge, to put it mildly. Still, the only alternative would seem to be despair. That is the most useless response of all. It teaches us nothing. We cannot learn from it. It is but a dark, airless pit into which our Will disappears without a trace.

It is my view that what is taking place in the world now is this. As the industrialized world exhausts its resources, its energy base in the broad sense (soils, forests, oil, cheaply mined ores, clean water, fisheries, clean air and the rest), and prices rise accordingly, the great, grand myths that were the ideological superstructure of that world, the myths of endless progress and rational human perfectibility, slowly begin to loosen and break up. The "developed" world, which is where these myths thrived and gave us so much dynamism and power, begins to fall apart, both energetically and as a body of convictions. So-called "post-modernism," an era saturated with doubt, arrives.

This is not an uncommon sort of thing in regional human history, this break-up of empire. When it happens complex institutions begin to settle toward simpler levels, levels where non-rational (I do not say anti-rational) processes are sovereign. This is what I will refer to as a "return to the shadows." The "shadows" is the place where new myths and new taboos rule, a place where new definitions of what is good and what is not come into being. Some of these beliefs are emotionally satisfying, others repugnant, noxious inventions of messianic leaders. All sorts of "instant traditions" may appear, like those invented by Nazism, Maoism and communism. Political systems molt and emerge as bizarre religious systems. War lords squabble and midnight assassinations disturb the night.

At other times this return to the shadows can be a long and tormented unwinding of the past. "There is a lot of ruin in an empire" as some statesman somewhere put it. Recall the engravings of Giovanni Piranesi, those haunting images of crumbling aqueducts and once mighty vaulted halls of ancient Rome with their eighteenth century urban peasants' hovels huddling among the ruins? The great triumphal parades are gone, but so are the hideous slaughters at the coliseum. Roman law has evaporated, or was transmogrified. Slavery, on the other hand, never really disappeared. The question then looms, of course, is whether or not "the shadows" are but grey, filthy, infernal places such as William Hogarth's engravings show us, places where people fend off misery and madness with gin, opium and hangings.

Will "the shadows" be a place where healthy social life is possible and laughter can also be heard? Certainly many tribal peoples of the recent past, the Australian aborigines, and Amazon Indians and Mbutu pygmy seem to have once laughed a good deal and lived healthy social lives, give or take some unappealing habits such as head hunting and male subincision.

When we watch a television documentary showing Nazi SS men, immaculately dressed, tugging primly at the wrists of their gloves as they move about among concentration camp victims, compulsively counting and recounting inmates about to be shot or gassed, does not the most rational among us agree that human rationality is often displayed in a strikingly elliptical fashion? So are we witnessing, even now amidst all the talk of ever greater exploits by the "developed" world, a troubling unease and a haunting sense of "sin" the modernist mind had thought it banished long ago?

When told of the obliteration of Hiroshima and Nagasaki, J. Robert Oppenheimer, the physicist at the center of the vast American atomic bomb building project, the Manhattan Project, supposedly concluded, gloomily one can presume, that "Physicists have known sin and this is a knowledge they cannot forget." This belated epiphany is the more striking when set alongside what a fellow physicist is supposed to have said of Oppenheimer after the first atomic test-bomb was exploded at Almagordo. "His walk was like [the hero of the movie] *High Noon*. He had done it!"

I do not wish to pick on Oppenheimer, and I am not interested here in the debate about whether he or Enrico Fermi, or others, were letting the Russians in on the secrets of the bomb in the naive belief that it might allay Stalin's worries, or soften his heart, or speed the emptying of Gulag camps. What is significant for our purposes is that Oppenheimer apparently had suddenly grasped the thought that physicists, for all their rationalist posturing, could invent things in the name of science and live to regret the costs, the "sin," that inevitably accompanied their use. It was as if he saw suddenly that "pure" research was but a fiction, that any "truth" has meaning only as a use.

Edward Teller adds this to the Oppenheimer story, speaking to a National Academy of Sciences symposium on July 16, 1995, "I blame others for spreading too much fear [about the bomb]," not Oppenheimer, who had quoted lines at Almagordo from the Bragavadgita, "Now I am become Death, the destroyer of worlds."

"I wish," said Teller, "he had said something entirely different. ... We scientists have done our job. ... Now ... it is up to everyone in the body politic to apply that knowledge to world events in a positive way."

And an interesting footnote to the first test was added by William Laurence of The New York Times. He was present at the first test explosion at Almagordo. "Dr. Bethe and I discussed [while awaiting the countdown] his epochal discovery of the thermonuclear reactions that power the sun and stars. For me it was a memorable dialogue: we were about to witness the first massive fission explosion, yet we talked of controlled fusion--the steady burning of hydrogen in stars. We pointedly did not discuss the prospect of future H-bombs, also based on thermonuclear reactions."

Now, as they say in motion picture making, cut to the scene with the rabbi and the monk. The Jewish father Rabbi Haddarsham claimed that human nature was contaminated by an "evil leaven" and he claimed that "The imagination of man's heart is evil from its youth." And I am sure there are few, if any, cultures in the world that do not hold one version or another of this view of human nature, that it is unpredictable, given to excess and easily perverted. The nature of evil, after all, is what the whole tangled debate we call theology is mostly about.

In Christendom the point has been hammered away at for centuries. Blaise Pascal, a remarkable man of religion, mathematics and science, living but a short life, from 1623 to 1662, with one foot in the medieval past and the other in the emerging modern age, makes the point in his famous *Pensees*. Setting the trap as deftly as it has ever been set, he asks, "And how should [original sin] be perceived by reason, since it is a thing against reason, and since reason, far from finding out her own ways, is averse to it when it is presented to her."

What this boils down to, if one can presume to "boil down" the laconic wisdom of Pascal, is that modern man, especially modern rationalist man, harbors a deep resentment of his own limits. He prefers to assume, reasonably he believes, of course, that there are no limits on his reason. For, needless to say, the idea that reason is self-limiting by virtue of its inevitable flaws and vainglory, which are costs, or that mankind must share a planet of finite space and resources with species we assume are less wise, certainly less thoughtful, has profound implications for the place of non-reason in our lives.

These implications open an entire, new set of problems for the next century. For if Pascal is correct, and I believe he is, reason is ringed about by a vast expanse of non-reasoned human experience, a virtual kingdom that lies in "the shadows" of unquestioned habit. It follows, moreover, that reason's hegemony over great areas of what we call "reality" is far more tenuous than we like to think. Further, if the costs of our rationalist pomps are hidden from us, if we are "averse" to even recognizing them, we are doomed inevitably to pay the piper when fundamental matters of man's place in nature arrive in the next century.

Let me intrude a point on the term "sin" to prevent the secular minded person from simply throwing this book aside. I wish to substitute the word "cost" for the word "sin," at least to avoid becoming enmeshed in a theological dispute, since most such disputes have inviting entrances but few exits. To paraphrase Pascal we might say, "Reason is averse to appreciating its own costs since her costs are her inherent limits."

We might label this the "Teller aversion syndrome," since he is so striking an example of the purblind claim of many scientists that "pursuing the truth for its own sake," that is, "pure science," is possible. The Teller aversion syndrome rests on the belief that there can be unmotived "pursuit" of truth, which, of course, is nonsense. Curiosity is a motive, vanity is a motive, money is a motive, fame is a motive. Living itself is a motive.

The term "sin" is troublesome, moreover, because it has always gotten so much attention in places in which wary modernists seldom set foot, in churches, synagogues and mosques. If they do take a chance and enter such places, in the belief that their reason might squeeze some meaning out of the whole business, they may be chided or excoriated by some pharisaic rabbi, lachrymose conman or gloomy priest for sins they (the unsuspecting rationalist) have never had chance to commit. And the issue of sin, after all, is often a question of opportunity. In any case, the idea of limits to reason, or the sinful use of reason, has been the topic of some of the greatest writing of the modernist world, *Faust* and *Frankenstein* for instance. So modern man can at least take credit for that, everyday crimes, war and perfidy set to one side.

But to return to the subject more directly again. I think it correct to say that the vast kingdom "of the shadows" constitutes most, almost all, of what we experience in daily life. It includes those strange, bewitching, banal, and sometimes repulsive human habits, such as rite, ritual, art, myth, music, courtship, body deformation, tattooing, games, play, comedy, theater, prayer, magic, fashion, fantasy, flag waving, worship of the stars, homage to the sun. None of these is rational in the strict sense. Yet many are shaped or driven by natural laws and biological regulators that lurk within them, most at bottom, ecological forces that are far more subtle than commonly appreciated. They are whatever it is that tempts us constantly to capitalize the word "Nature," no less instinctively than pre-literate people name the gods and spirits that constitute the natural order. They are probably not "Gaia" at work, but the fundamental biological order. I call this order "meta-rational." It operates "in the shadows."

In Max Oelschlaeger's fine book, published in 1991, *The Idea of Wilderness*, allusions to something similar to a meta-rationality in nature show up continuously, especially when he discusses the more mystical sides of John Muir and Aldo Leopold. What is missing is an exploration of the way the non-reasonable side of social life works.

But if Nature, including the vast landscape of human non-reason, rite, ritual, myth, music, art, ceremonialized courtship, warfare, cannibalism and the rest, is forever just outside the reach of reason, because of reason's hauteur, our efforts to extend the reach of the sciences, especially the social and psychological sciences, into these areas is a quixotic enterprise. That is why a "return to the shadows" poses the many paradoxes it does. The strange fatuity that has lurked about in the mythos of progress for centuries, that "pure" pursuit of knowledge is actually possible, reminds us just how brave, euphoric and naive this kind of thinking can be. There is actually a touching innocence about much of it.

Take, for instance, the thoughts of the historian Charles Beard. We find him writing in the introduction to J. B. Bury's famous *The Idea of Progress*, in 1931, that as technological progress sweeps mankind forward, "warriors, priests and political leaders sink into the background." He could not know then, of course, that Stalin, Hitler and the Japanese warlords had no intention of "sinking into the background."

But Beard announced something even more grand. He said that the idea of progress "differs from all fixed ideas of the past," and that it contains "the germs of infinite expansion." What Beard had gotten hold of was half of the principle of automatic control, now a commonplace in engineering and cybernetics. He had identified the notion of self-amplification, so-called positive feedback, and took it to apply to the idea of progress, an idea whose appetite feeds upon itself. He did not know, or appreciate, that the other half of the principle of automatic control is negative feedback, damping processes, by which a dynamic system brings itself to equilibrium or self-destructs, exhausting its resources, as an oil tanker fire might.

Alfred North Whitehead said something similar to what Beard says when he announced that the greatest invention of the nineteenth century was "the invention of the art of invention." Indeed, for almost three hundred years the air was thick with these beguiling beliefs.

Bruce Williams, in a review of Colin Norman's *The God that Limps: Science and Technology in the Eighties*, which appeared in 1982, makes note of the strange blind spot that so often accompanied these naive beliefs about the positive feedback features of our culture's life. For while we could boast of a future filled with great achievements, boasts that were realized, atomic power, moon rockets, incredible computers, potent new pesticides, and all the rest, we were "averse" to thoughts about the downside of these achievements, radioactive waste, budget-busting space projects, labor displacement because of computers, short-term gains with synthetic fertilizers, and the exhaustion of non-renewable resources such as oil. So that while the self-amplifying side of the "art of invention" was forecast well, the cost side of the equation, the negative feedback side, was missed almost completely. It ended up like the clutter on a cutting room floor in Hollywood, along with the other half-spent delusions and sins awaiting definition.

As I said, in the sciences, one of the myths that has attended the notion of "infinite expansion" is that there can be "pure" pursuit of knowledge "for its own sake," which is to say an unmotivated pursuit of truth. This myth rests on the same illusion that Beard clung to, that "infinite expansion" is actually possible. This despite the fact that common sense tells us that no living system, be it a colony of bacteria or a great economy, can expand indefinitely. But common sense is often, as we know, an uncommon thing.

The play of negative feedback processes explains to a large degree why the news is now so full of stories concerning social control, stories that frequently concern questions of taboos and the new need for them, some notion, at least, of "sin." So it is no surprise that *Newsweek*, for instance, ran a cover story in 1995 called "Shame," and that it included a one-page essay titled "What Ever Happened to Sin?" "Sin" had not been lost, of course, only our willingness to confront its reality, the "evil leaven" that people like Rabbi Haddarsham had been talking about over the ages.

What triggered the *Newsweek* piece, I am sure, is rampaging "sin" in American society, street crime, Wall Street crime, drug smuggling, child pornography, terrorism and the like. Many of these factors had been obscured in our society by the rhetoric of "freedom." But "freedom" is but one part of the equation for successful adaptation in the natural world. Constraint is the other.

Take the case of the 'sexual revolution." Here was a positive feedback phenomenon if there ever was one. It was presided over by all sorts of strange, gnomic television talk-doctors trying to tell people about everything from oral sex to migraines, or which might come first. Then AIDS arrived. The revolution turned into a pitiable debauch that festered in bathhouses and heroin needles. Negative feedback came into play. So much for that revolution.

And more recently, in June of 1995, the lead article in the *New York Times Magazine* was called "Evil's Back" and presented a lengthy "theological journey into the dark heart of

America," discussing everything from cases of parents murdering their children, children murdering their parents, and the 1995 Oklahoma City bombing. All of this, meanwhile, without the aid of Dr. Oppenheimer. It was as if the entire American society had found itself knee deep in the gummy muck of normlessness, alternatively terrified by its predicament and enraptured by the thrill of the ooze.

Which has put both conservative and liberal minds in a predicament. Should they understand "sin" or judge it? Conservatives, naturally enough, prefer to use tradition to avoid the discomfort of "understanding" it. After all, traditions come into existence as collective habits to meet just such predicaments. In principle, once a problem has been met, solved, judged, settled, it can be loaded into a tradition whose reason for being is to process judgments automatically. This saves the individual the psychic stress of going through what others have already gone through. That is why, indeed, societies are inherently conservative. The hazard of tradition, on the other hand, is that it often treats new problems as if they were old problems, and can pay a price for being wrong. That, of course, is why conservatives perseverate the way they do when habit lets them down.

Liberals face the opposite problems with "sin." To avoid having to judge it, they "understand" it, propping up their feckless posture with the old bromide, "To understand is to forgive." So they typically call in a psychologist or sociologist to help "understand" the causes of criminal acts, slothful behavior, brutal outrages, and nihilism generally. This has its price, too. All old problems are treated as if they were new problems. Stalin's crimes, for instance, are taken as something new or unforeseen, a special case of betrayal, rather than simply one more case of the cursed "evil leaven" at work, something inherent to absolutism, something to be judged "evil" automatically.

The same has come to apply to gunfights in the school ground or campus incubated politically correct outrages. "Every case is different!" goes the cant, when, in fact, every case is the same as every other of the same kind. Thus categories of "evil" are not allowed to come into existence, and it is impossible to judge them routinely. And so the conservative and the liberal take turns standing each other's argument upside down, the better to avoid dealing with things right side up.

Let me comment briefly on a point of importance I will enlarge on later. Cultures are essentially information banks. Their structure is a record of their experience. So they are predictor systems as well. What we call "traditions" are habit structures that are supposed to tell us what to do, how to optimize our successes and minimize our failures. Each is what John B. Calhoun, the biologist, calls an "ideomass," stored information, most of which operates on a non-conscious level.

The so-called "modern world" is just such a structure, an enormous body of information compacted into our beliefs and usages, such as economic, political and religious traditions. The "modern world" is overlaid, of course, with a vast international web of corporate and political bureaucracies. They are, in principle, rationally governable, though we all know that is largely an illusion. But they are, in sum, a sort of empire.

But the modernist empire is very complex and very fragile. A serious shock to one part of it is a serious shock to all of it. It is what one anthropologist, Kent Flannery, would call "hypercoherent." Damage or infection in one part of it and the entire system, the "global village" we hear so much about, is in trouble.

A fictional case in point. A suburbanite in, say, Columbus, Ohio, sits about the club where he plays golf, mouthing the expected conservative political platitudes of his sub-culture, as he plans a vacation with his well-groomed trophy wife to see the famed ruins in Luxor, Egypt.

As they return to their river boat after visiting the ruins, a God-fearing Muslin with a rapid-fire rifle smuggled in from the Sudan, shoots them both dead, on the grounds that Allah will save Egypt from poverty and corruption, not these boozy tourists he sees dismounting from luxury river boats up from Cairo.

Suddenly both conservatives from Columbus are major players on the international scene. Fax machines whir and grunt. CNN runs a special on tourist hunting and interviews a movie star just recovered from being shot by a fanatic in storied Samarkand. The Presidency of Egypt is in a stew over Muslim fundamentalist threats. Poverty-ridden urban peasants roaming the alleys of Cairo are caught up in angry debates over the need for tourism and the ruin of traditional flood-plain agriculture on the Nile because of the high dam that was sponsored by a Soviet nation that no longer exists. And since shooting tourists hurts tourism in Egypt, and hard currency exchange rates, there is much cheek clucking in the State Department over foreign aid debates erupting in the U.S. Senate. Much of the Middle East is absorbed yet again in fierce debates about what the Prophet may or may not have said in the Koran about shooting people from places like Columbus, Ohio. The entire hypercoherent "global village" vibrates from end to end.

But as philosophers are fond of saying, "Seeing requires distance." So it is useful at this point to look at historical events of the last few centuries as they flow along the streambed of cause and effect, doubling back too in odd swirls and eddies of the unexpected. The Eighteenth Century's Enlightenment was one of those remarkable swirls or eddies, full of the froth of high expectation, set off too by pools of remarkable philosophic clarity and insight. A brief look at some of its features will help me make my case.

Chapter 2

Elegant Amnesia

Beginning, more or less, with the mid-seventeenth century many Western thinkers attempted to deal with the problem of the "evil leaven" by a truly remarkable intellectual exploit. They attempted nothing less than to disown memory, and history as memory, to make "war on the ancients" of the classic world, such as Homer, Ovid, Livy and Virgil. To many of the eighteenth century, the historical record was little more than a "code of fraud and woe," "a disgrace to humanity, every page being crowded with crimes and follies." The Enlightenment assumed the form of elegant amnesia.

J. B. Bury's *The Idea of Progress*, and Sidney Pollard's book of the same name, outline this story compellingly. And with equal interest and perhaps with more grace, so does Carl Becker's *The Heavenly City of the Eighteenth-Century Philosophers.*[*]

---

[*]I might note in passing that the term "progress" is said to have derived from Anne-Robert Jacques Turgot's famous lecture "On the Successive Advances of the Human Mind," delivered at the Sorbonne in December of 1750. Many other figures, Helvetius, Condorcet and Godwin among them, also wrote a good deal at

Collective memory can be construed to take two forms at that time. One was, as I said, the record as set down by the ancients. Men such as Jean D'Alembert, for example, was an astute mathematician and contributor to Diderot's famed *Encyclopedie*. He is said to have "felt a sort of resentment of history" and to have called for the burning of the historical record.

The other form that collective memory took was contained in "original sin," the core of the Christian model of man. Ernst Cassirer, the 20th century philosopher, says that the one thing that all of the great thinkers of the Enlightenment agreed upon was the concept of "original sin." They detested it. It lay, they felt, like a giant, sullen boulder of superstition across the path of progress of reasoning mankind.

What is notable about "original sin," however, is that it is a powerful, sanctified metaphor that performs what anthropologists call a "summarizing function." It rolls into a single phrase an entire set of traditional beliefs, myths, and rituals. It is as if a vast record of human experience, in this case with the dark side of human nature, had jelled into a compact set of habits, those "rules active in us" as the American philosopher Charles S. Peirce called habit. When they become traditionalized, these habits, "rules active in us," represent what historical consciousness represents, except that they represent a particular form of information encoded in social structures and functions, memory without consciousness.

I would like to enlarge briefly on this point. To many information theorists, structure and information are the same thing. "Learning is any receipt of information," according to Gregory Bateson. So that we may say that as a cultural structure

---

that time about human perfectibility. But Aleksandr Solzhenitsyn, in a recent cranky interview, laid most of the blame for the idea on Turgot. But as we like to say in politics these days, "There is enough blame to go around."

On the other hand, if one were forced to take sides on the period Turgot wrote about, most of us, having read Simon Schama's superb book on the French Revolution, *Citizens*, would find it a tough call. The quest for human perfectibility can be a bloody business.

takes form it "learns." "Institutions" are complex systems of habit, many of which are co-dependent roles. Such habits allow people to process information without needless repetition, avoiding the psychological costs of solving every problem from scratch. Denying us our habits would be like denying us our sleep.

Barbara Tuckman, in *The Distant Mirror*, reminds us that medieval man's belief in "original sin" ran deep for very good reason. For one thing, it helped explain the senseless misery of everyday life. It also helped account for life in filthy hovels infested with plague, food that was often chewed with abscessed teeth screaming with pain, and, of course, the death of children in the cradle. It helped account for brutish wars, atrocities and the greed of people in power. It even helped account for temptations in the market place. Saint Augustine had said that "Business is in itself evil." St. Jerome said the same: "A man who is a merchant can seldom please God." While neither saint would find himself welcome at a Chamber of Commerce meeting, the point is that this view of the dark side of our being processes information. It was why, Tuckman says, medieval laws tried at times to prevent underselling, the use of child labor, false advertisement, even the use of artificial light.

The same sort of thing was sometimes done with warfare. Medieval rules of battle would then call for warring parties to agree upon a place of battle, a place where knights were able to "unfurl their banners" and go about their butchery in a relatively formal way. These chivalric rules reduced the role of lower class infantry and their cruder, unpredictable reactions to killing. Of course this did not happen often or last for long. The Crusades, especially as they involved masses of rabble in a holy war illustrate what could happen when chivalric ritual broke down. Some of the crusaders, cross in one hand and an axe in the other, committed random atrocities against Christian cities as well as infidel strongholds. At times these less than chivalrous fellows actually engaged in cannibalism, evidently to stave off famine.

But we can also observe that the rules that now and then appeared in those times were more than a matter of humane behavior.   They resemble the rules of battle that animals commonly apply to regulate breeding rights, to avoid lethal fights by shifting the emphasis in conflict to rules of space and hierarchy.*

Some Renaissance Italian mosaics and frescoes illustrate how information about "sin" was processed, reminding sinners what to expect if they did not mend their ways. The lustful are thrown into fire, the gluttonous eat their own flesh, the slothful become stray bones too lazy to recombine for resurrection, a bloated Satan eats and then defecates sinners, a sodomist is reamed on a spit through the anus. This sort of thing is, in fact, a negative feedback display in what may be called the social cybernetics of "sin."

But let us return to the philosophes and their attitude toward the establishment, the Church in particular. Their attitudes toward this old institution are not difficult to understand, considering some of the outlandish things that the Church expected its followers to swallow. It was not just a matter of the voluptuous use of wealth, or even the torture chambers of such men as the Archbishop of Salzburg, which we may visit to this day. It was not even the devilishly inspired sophistries of such writers as Joseph d'Maistre, making the case for continued use by the Church of force and every sort of degenerate torture. It was also such things as expecting innocent church-goers to worship the supposed foreskin of Jesus at three different sites in France

---

*And it is useful to note that the controlling influence of chivalric rules on warfare was not confined to Europe. Noel Perrin, in his 1979 book GIVING UP THE GUN notes how the samurai classes in medieval Japan, revering long years of training for ritualized combat, slowed the use of the gun for almost three hundred years. The gun could be used, after all, by riff-raff as easily as by knights. But as Pascal might have warned, it takes but a single commander contaminated by the "evil leaven," who says to hell with the rules and goes for all-out victory, to upset the apple cart. Which is why the gun came to Japanese warfare.

at the same time. Needless to say, sharp minds like Voltaire's and Thomas Paine's had a field day with these absurdities.

And there was always the Jesuit order with its literary censors, its bullying arrogance and unblushing defense of authoritarianism. It was the sort of thing that Joseph II of Austria took a stand against during the Enlightenment, often on behalf of the man on the street, especially the rising new bourgeoisie who demanded freedom not only in the marketplace but in the library. Joseph remains one of those figures from the Enlightenment we tend to overlook because of our focus on events in France and England.

Bury also makes the point that one of the causes of the intense resentment of the philosophes with the old ecclesiastical order was the shock of the Copernican revolution. It represented, he says, a traumatic dislodgment of mankind, and his earth, from the center of the universe. Rationalist thinkers had little choice, he says, but to treat this humiliation as a kind of deliverance from old theistic superstitions, to put forward the best scientific interpretation of mankind's new situation.

The disgrace that many felt because of Copernicus' discoveries was compounded later, of course, by the Darwinian revolution. Mankind and his earth were not only knocked out of the center of the cosmic theater, it was no longer obvious that mankind was created in the image of God. So it made, in its own way, good sense to reinterpret mankind more resolutely from a humanist and scientific point of view. And in our own time, creationists try to deal with the mountain of scientific evidence on evolution by simply lurching into the welcoming arms of denial.

Sidney Pollard, on the other hand, stresses that much of the rationalistic change of the 16th, 17th and 18th centuries was powered by the rise of the bourgeoisie and a thousand big and little practical inventions that had more to do with marketplace needs than with philosophic niceties or well-turned phrases in the salons. He is doubtlessly correct to a very great extent. The rise of the idea of progress had a very pedestrian side to it.

James Burke's television series *Connections* does a splendid job tracing this sort of thing. So too does the Arts and Entertainment television series on the biographies of famous industrialists such as the Kelloggs, Hersheys and DuPonts. These men were less concerned with what Kant or Spinoza might have thought about pure reason or the relationship of mind and matter. They were concerned with inventing a better corn flake, chocolate bar or explosive. And they demanded the freedom from government to do it. In a nutshell, in fact, this is what bourgeois demands for total "freedom," even today, are all about.

But all of these events flow in and out of one another, form pools and eddies in the historical flow. Still, while one great scientific discovery and one technological invention followed upon another, all of it took place at the expense of "history" as the ancients had laid it out, or as religious ideas such as "original sin" summed it up. Which is why, in recent times, James Joyce's Stephen Daedelus was to say that "History is a nightmare from which I am trying to awake." Why, too, Henry Ford, more to the point, more American if you like, simply concluded that history was "bunk."

This desire to replace history, which many philosophes saw as something like an old newspaper, full of useless stories of muggings, murders and mayhem, with something more uplifting, took form as the idea of "progress." The old interpretation of mankind's voyage through the tempest of life, which ended hopefully when he came ashore in heaven, "original sin" dragging along behind him like some weedy theological sea anchor, was pushed aside in favor of an up-beat, progressive vision of a new paradise on earth. Needless to say again, market forces, imperialism, and the rise of a new bourgeoisie added class consciousness and explosive resentments of a new kind to the mix.

Interestingly enough, but expectable too, all these emerging ideas about everlasting progress took many twists and turns in educational philosophy. Almost without exception they too were progressive in their view of a child's presumed natural goodness and perfectibility. Many of the reforms that followed were, to be sure, long overdue, such as with the Swiss reformer Johann Pestalozzi who lived from 1746 to 1827, and ran a school for poor children, and Frederick Froebel who lived from 1782 to 1852. Froebel founded the kindergarten movement. These men removed a lot of the cruelty and pointless rigidity from primary education.

So too it was later with John Dewey. But interestingly enough his "child-centered" education was in its own way a "war against the ancients." In Dewey's system, the memory bank that we refer to as "adult experience" is treated as a hobble on the natural unfolding of the child's potential. Dewey's *School and Society*, published in 1899, and its "learn by doing" principles, his "experimentalism," soon became cant amongst primary school educators. Its anti-historical, or at least ahistorical, slant should not be missed. The "learn by doing" principle implies that sensation in the moment is as important as memory of the past. Children experience; adults remember.

Which is why Dewey recommended, for instance, that children learn about weaving cloth by weaving cloth, not just reading about weaving cloth. Which sounds valid and exciting enough, until one considers that the history of cloth-making is very old and very complex and cannot possibly be recapitulated in a child's hands-on experience. And in the vocabulary of what became known as "progressive education" the teacher became known as "the first learner" in the classroom, which meant essentially that the teacher was thought of as another child, a creature with a shallow past.

In the process the teacher, as memory, experience, becomes what Henry Ford called history, "bunk." In other words, collective memory stored in traditions or social structure, as information, became pitted against sensation. Sensation is set against memory. And in many schools this elegant amnesia gave way to crude amnesia, to Ford's "bunk," and often an active resentment for the study of history of any sort. Which deprives the student of what John Kotre, in his 1996 study of memory, *White Gloves: How We Create Ourselves Through Memory*, calls "positive illusions," models of what he or she ought to be, robbing them of what Kotre calls "ancestral help." And the less we know about the past's dark side, the easier it is to be an optimist about the future. This may explain, in part certainly, why unrepentant optimists are often controlling personalities who demand we share their smiles and denials no matter what the evidence.

The optimism of the seventeenth century was not totally new, to be sure. Even with things as bad as they always seemed to be, Desiderius Erasmus could still say in 1518, that "at present I could almost wish to be rejuvenated for a few years, for this reason, that I believe I see a golden age dawning in the near future." But man is a slow learner, so we may forgive Erasmus' heirs if they failed to see how chimerical his visions.

Of course, normal human beings must to some degree forget pain, or compact it for easier handling into a sanctified metaphor such as "original sin," or they will be overwhelmed by its memory and perhaps go mad. That may explain, in part at any rate, why men like the eighteenth century's Reverend Joseph Priestly, the discoverer of oxygen, and a man of considerable prestige, could have his house and laboratory burned by neighbors because he showed too much sympathy for the French Revolution, then flee to America and continue to speak of the "paradisiacal future" of the human race.

But there is something profoundly sad about the kind of optimism that buoyed great minds of that period. Take the case of the eighteenth century's Marquis de Condorcet. A philosopher and mathematician prominent in his day, he sided with the Girondists, moderates of the French Revolution, many of whom the radical wing had executed. Condorcet was driven into hiding, hid out for a while in the forest and was finally captured and imprisoned. All the while he continued to ponder the perfectibility of man, as if he had not been soured by his ordeal. Unfortunately he is said to have died under suspicious circumstances in prison. Alas, the trouble with optimism is that it is, all too often, a poor predictor.

Chapter 3

The First True Post-Modern

The Enlightenment was a very special time in the West. It was a time when Joseph Priestly could dilate on the future "all glorious and paradisiacal." About the same time, Adam Ferguson, prominent too, and given to deep, rationalistic surmises, concluded that man was "formed with a general disposition to affect what he conceives to be good." And William Godwin, whom J. B. Bury says hated government as much or more than any of his time, was compelled to announce, "Once establish the perfectibility of man, and it will inevitably follow that we are advancing to a state in which truth will be too well known to be easily mistaken." Ironically enough, Godwin was the father of Mary Shelley, author of *Frankenstein*. William could have learned from Mary.

In that series of lectures by Carl Becker in 1931, published as *The Heavenly City of the Eighteenth-Century Philosophers*, Becker makes the point that even as the high optimism of the Enlightenment was reaching its zenith, doubts began to creep into their thoughts about the sovereignty of Reason: "... when the Goddess pointed to her judgments, the Philosophers, almost without exception, refused to accept them; instead of looking at the writing on the wall, they turned their backs and edged away, giving one excuse or other."

Not everyone at the time was an unconditional optimist, to be sure, certainly not the likes of Voltaire. And Jeremy Bentham, the great utilitarian, saw perfect happiness as something as illusive as the "universal elixir and philosopher's stone." And there are many striking illustrations in Becker's splendid little book of the way thinkers struggled with the paradox of human nature, its good will and its dark side.

According to Becker, David Hume, the great Scottish skeptic, a man who had as fine a mind as existed at that or any other time, renowned for his cast-iron arguments indicating that we do not experience cause, only correlation, set to writing his famed *Dialogues Concerning Natural Religion*, published in 1779, three years after his death. It is said he came away with such a gloomy assessment of a universe from which Reason had banished God that he kept the manuscript locked in his desk and turned, late in life, to his earlier religious beliefs.

It was not long until writers like Thomas Carlyle began acting as if rationalism's failings had seared their very souls. Carlyle began to see a world "all void of Life, Purpose, of volition, even of Hostility; it is one huge, dead, immeasurable Steam-engine, rolling on, in its dead indifference, to grind me limb from limb." And almost in despair he cries out, "Always there is a black spot in our sunshine; it is even, as I said, the Shadow of Ourselves." And he attempted to throw light into that Dark Spot by idealization of Great Men, Heroes, and the virtues of Work.

At the height of the Enlightenment, Reason, in its struggle against ignorance and superstition, was also dissolving tradition of a broader sort. It was generating the "irritation of doubt" that Charles Peirce, writing in the 1870s, said was the result of a "privation of habit." Peirce, the founder of pragmatism, had other fish to fry. But his were pivotal ideas that would come into their own in the twentieth century only too often to be grievously misused by latter-day "pragmatists" who did not understand the vital inertial guidance functions of either habit or tradition.

But one of the people who stands out in a unique way during the time when the "Shadow of Ourselves" began to cause so much "irritation of doubt" is Thomas Malthus, author of the famed 1798 *Essay on the Principle of Population*. In it he argued, it will be recalled, that human populations grow much faster than their food supply, unless checked by war, famine and disease, or by "moral" checks such as birth control by abstinence. Others, such as Marquis de Condorcet had identified much the same phenomenon, but according to Bury, did not have the nerve to come to grips with its implications. And to this day it is difficult for liberal thinkers who claim to love the common man to conclude that there are too many of them.

Malthus was a minister, as were many of the leading thinkers of that time, but also a decent person, not the grump whom his critics like to make him out to be. He had studied famine, did not wince, and had come to grips with one of the most basic of all laws of limitation, the number of people that can be loaded onto the planet.

It was not just the new reality Malthus was pointing to that makes so many uneasy or hostile. It was the fact that Malthus struck a fundamental blow to the grand myths of progress and human perfectibility. He posed the idea of limits in a way no one had had the nerve to do before.

So when William Godwin made the panglossian assertion that "There is no person who does not see how very distant such a period of [overpopulation] is from us," Malthus pulled him up short, by the scruff of Godwin's optimistic, philosophic neck. Malthus replied, "The period when the number of men surpasses their means of easy subsistence has long since arrived."

It is this riposte to Godwin that marks Malthus, in my opinion, as the first true post-modern, the first person to come to grips seriously with the one issue that will not go away, the inherent limits that the size of the planet and its basic resources, good soil, forests, fisheries and fresh water most notably, set on the number of human beings that can live on it with anything close to a decent quality of life.

What Malthus' work presaged is a profound revolution at the modernist foundation of our culture. It was the beginning of a basic shift in both thinking and behavior, nothing less than a major paradigm change. Thomas Kuhn outlines this kind of change in his well-known 1970 study, *The Structure of Scientific Revolutions*. Kuhn was not the first to identify the framework of such changes; others, John Dewey in philosophy, Herbert Simon in industrial management analysis and Anthony Wallace in anthropology, among others, have all set their ideas within the pioneering framework on the subject of problem-solving by Charles Peirce. But Kuhn's ideas are particularly relevant here. Although they concerned science, he defined a paradigm more broadly as a sort of model, as "the entire constellation of beliefs, values, techniques, and so on, shared by a given community." Each culture, in other words, is a paradigm, each a sort of sociological species that stores information in its customs, habits, and usages. Its success over the long haul depends on its strategic use of this stored information.

Kuhn notes that in the sciences ideas do not develop in a linear, sequential accumulation of ideas but in a much more haphazard, unplanned sort of way. Periods of relatively quiet change take place, followed by the appearance of "anomalies" that cannot be understood, and produce stress, within the established framework of scientific thinking. They may be followed by a radical shift in theory to accommodate the discordancy.

It is my contention that Malthus' work on population represented an "anomaly" within the progress thinking of the modern culture and that present neo-Malthusian ideas indicate that a major paradigm shift is underway.

In fact, one of the great central anomalies of our time is what the biologist Garrett Hardin identified in 1968 as a global "Tragedy of the Commons." He argued that we cannot maximize the number of people living on the planet and their standard of living at the same time. He concluded that "relinquishing the freedom to breed" is now an imperative and that it can best be accomplished by "mutual coercion mutually agreed upon."

"Mutual coercion mutually agreed upon," would represent, of course, a very radical paradigm shift. It is, in fact, unlikely. Hardin observes that the "morality of an act is a function of the state of the system at the time it is performed." And he is obviously correct. The morality of a solitary "mountain man" urinating in a mountain stream is different from the morality of an entire town or city doing the same thing. But the question then is, "What is the state of the post-modern paradigm at the present time?"

A single paradigm, or sets of them, with an over-arching general paradigm, such as a "culture" represents, need not shift or collapse all at once. In fact, the shock of change may not set in until well after the first tremor. In an ironic sense the denial thinking that I alluded to earlier, especially among conservatives who find it impossible to imagine a world radically different from what they are used to, is an indication of just how much pressure is building along the Malthusian fault line. Indeed the stress that is building in the post-modernist world because of neo-Malthusian thinking is often most obvious in the denial it triggers.

Unlike critics who announce airily that "Malthus has been proved wrong!"--citing usually some short-lived success in raising food production here or there about the world to head off a famine--Malthus would not blink at the realities before him. The issue remained a question of the long term, not the short term. And the core of the problem was human breeding habits.

The reader may recall the highly touted "green revolution" some years ago and the fact that it did raise food production dramatically in some places. And agriculturalists regularly announce such "revolutions in food productions," some "agricultural breakthrough." But populations immediately explode in response to such "green revolutions" and the result is that more people end up facing new famines than faced old ones. The present slowing of world population growth which the United Nations reports, is all well and good, but something resembling an ecological population crash would seem to be a more probable requirement, if "requirement" is the word, for significant population adjustment to occur, if "adjustment" is the word.

Another indication of the fact that things are already out of control is the denial thinking of some social scientists. Some used to talk, some still do, about a "demographic transition" that would take place across the world as nations "developed." This idea says basically that when economic standards of living rise high enough people have fewer children, presumably because they are then liberated from assorted superstitions about the importance of having very large families, and are more selfishly caught up in being consumers.

This sort of argument is heard, for instance, in connection with China's "new prosperity." But there is very little evidence that population growth over most of the planet is not, in fact, still accelerating at an ominous rate. Unwelcome though the thought may be, places like Haiti, Somalia, the Gaza Strip and Nigeria are probably better indicators of what the future holds for most of mankind than are the wishes of happy little islands of plenty still found in the "developed world."

Wole Soyinka's recent book about Nigeria, called *The Open Sore of a Continent*, in which he notes, for instance, that Nigeria's one hundred million population is doubling every twenty-two years, is just one more case in point. So is Robert Kaplan's recent *The Ends of the Earth*, which recounts his recent travels through West Africa, Egypt, Turkey, Iran, the southern states of the former Soviet Union, India and points east. It is not a reassuring report.

And oddly enough, one of the tragedies of the environmental movement itself is that it is as much a symptom as a cure for all of this, an "anomaly" in the Kuhnian sense within "development" thinking. This accounts too for the intense hostility with which environmentalists are so often met, by people in the affluent economic classes as well as amongst workers such as loggers and fishermen. Hence the sort of outraged double-think logic we see in groups such as Wise Use here in the United States. This despite the fact that something like seventy percent of the Western world's population call themselves environmentalists.

Still, I do not think pessimism is actually the normal state of the human temperament. In a certain sense, hope is built into us biologically, rather like the impulse to pray. The trick is to use our rational side while still distrusting it, to be a realist knowing that the price may be pain, disappointment, even betrayal. That, after all, is where courage begins.

But consider some of the evidence, especially the ancient claim of such wise men as the Greek philosophers, that man is a rational animal. Lay that claim alongside Frederick Morton's fine book *Thunder at Twilight*, published a few years ago. It describes the delirious joy with which street crowds in Vienna, London and Berlin greeted declarations of war between the royal families of Europe in 1914. Here was an entire generation, with the exception, of course, of the venerated royal families themselves, stampeding toward the ghastly, blood-soaked horrors of the trenches in France and Russia. It was as if the masses were fearful that their mad lemming-like charge toward the abyss might be halted at any moment by an unwelcome outburst of common sense.

There is perhaps no more compelling an account of that grisly abyss than that given us by Robert Graves' famous *Goodbye to All That*. Unfortunately, Graves' memoir of life in the trenches, or others like it, have not proven to be the antidote that some hoped they would to the viruses of jingoism and giddy rationalistic optimism.

And reading and rereading history does not make things easier. It tends to make misanthropes of us, even if we have happy home lives, or incline us at least to understand why Voltaire became famous for his sardonic smile when asked his opinion of human nature. Indeed, one is tempted to speculate that had Voltaire not possessed his notorious sense of humor he would have ended up throwing himself off a bridge into a river, after the manner of Munch's creature's apparent intention. For incredible though it seems, and contrary to what the rational animal dearly wishes at times were not so, humankind often seems less to abhor war, violence and depravity than to relish them.

It is easy to say, of course, that our gruesome habits are evidence that the entire human species has simply gone insane. But that is actually difficult to prove, largely because good, pacifistic people show up now and then and at times make a good case. Or we might assume that some primordial love of combat, contest, torture and trophy-taking has suddenly hypertrophied in the modern brain, like a tumor suddenly gone out of control. The fact is that mankind has been at the business of combat, willful destruction, torture and infamy for about as long as ancient bones can tell us. Some experts assert that in recorded global history peace has reigned across the entire planet for as long as twelve years at a stretch. Unfortunately for our present image, at the moment there are some twenty odd wars of assorted kinds going on.

One explanation for the situation, the simplest and probably the least ornately self-servingly pious, seems quite obvious. As populations have grown and technology has developed, the ferocity of war, genocide and perfidy, as well as the civic corruption that nests within these unsightly habits, has grown at what seems an almost geometric rate. Small populations and simple technological ways have their merits if for no better reason than that modesty is often built into them. Ernst Schumacher claimed rather much the same for economic habits when he published *Small is Beautiful* back in 1973.

Of course, a lot of this is hard to prove. Ancient populations can only be estimated and records of war and torture, such as we might find in paintings of the Mayans, Egyptians, or Chinese, are not meant to be statistical texts. But it does seem at times rather obvious that population density is a key to a good portion of the story. The Aztec could not have mounted days of mass human sacrifice had there not been enough people of other tribes around to capture and sacrifice en masse. Nor could the Romans have refined the arts of mass brutality against humans and animals had there not been enough Romans around to put together large armies of conquest.

So the rule (I hesitate to elevate it to the status of a "natural law") goes something like this. If humans collide, over a piece of meat, a sack of grain, a piece of land, women, anything, and they have clubs, they will use the clubs. Replace the club with a gun, and the gun will be used. Replace the gun with a bomb, and the bomb will be used. Call the tribe a neighborhood, enlarge the neighborhood to a nation, provide more people to participate, and the clubbing, shooting, and dismembering will intensify. So will the conceits and deceits that go with it. Put space enough between the opponents and the clubbing, shooting and dismembering will subside. So will the chicanery and knavish ways that go with it. In other words, if the population is thin enough, peace will prevail, a kind of left-handed "goodness." Great armies and great slaughters are unknown amongst the Australian aborigines. So also among Eskimo. And from what I have read of them, both peoples are decent people most of the time. This does not mean, on the other hand, that "small" and "good" are synonyms.

On the other hand, according to Peter Balakian, writing about the life and times of the painter Arshile Gorky, in the journal *Art in America*, in 1996, genocide in our century is to a good extent a technological achievement. The killing of over a million Armenians by the Ottoman government, this century's first great genocide, was systematically set in motion by the Turkish Minister of the interior, Talaat Pasha, with a telegram to various subordinates in 1916. In fact, Gerard Prunier, in his recent *The Rwanda Crisis: History of a Genocide*, is bold enough to say, "Genocides are a modern phenomenon--they require organization--and they are likely to become more frequent in the future." Though I think this may sell short some of our ancient ancestors, Tamerlane for one, he does have a point.

My reading of the evidence suggests then, that evil among humans on the grand scale is what ecologists might call "density dependent." This may sound much too straight forward for some to swallow. Certainly it does not let human nature off the hook. Which would make such a proposition very hard for some social scientists to put up with. And I have known social scientists, good people, often happily married people, often people who give to charities without coercion at their offices, who have spent most of their professional careers trying to prove that "war is not in our genes." But this is certainly a precarious argument whose chief merit seems to be that it helps us get our sleep.*

However, if we argue that evil on a grand scale (one is tempted to risk saying "a biblical scale") is density dependent, the obverse would seem to follow. If we turn the proposition inside out, or invert it, "goodness" also becomes density dependent. And that idea is an invitation to sentimental sophistry as arresting as anything that ever sent Jean Jacques Rousseau stumbling over his romanticist philosophic shoelaces.

So a misanthrope in good standing will not settle for a simple claim that "war is not in our genes," nor that evil tyrants account for all the trouble. That leaves too much out of consideration. Munch's creature would remind us of those vast armies of serfs, slaves and inmates in the Gulag, in Nazi camps and prison hell-holes around the world. He, or she (since misanthropes, as far as I know, come in both sexes), would also remind us of workers living like draft animals in a thousand and one free-enterprise sweat shops across the planet. He or she would remind us of the lives of great masses of people living in "misery belt" shanty-towns encircling most of the world's large "third world" cities. He, or she, will point to those offal and urine-contaminated gutters in which half-starved children can be photographed at play. He or she will point to those photographs of Rwandan bodies polluting rivers and lakes of East Africa as they rot. The "pangas," i.e., machetes, that killed them, Gerard Prunier would remind us, were mass produced in Chinese factories for export. Not all of these machetes were intended to cut brush or weeds in Rwandan gardens.

I do not make these observations because they provide some sort of perverse pleasure, though I realize some readers will

---

*Those intrested in the remorseless absurdity of war should see Qwynne Dyer's unflinching book, *War*, 1985, or the Public Broadcasting System television series out of which it grew. Dyer was the narrator of the PBS production.

insist that is so. I wish merely to stress the fact that there are costs to "development" and to "growth" and to insist that in nature a population explosion of any species sets natural correctives going. So the "tragedy of the commons" anomaly implies that some sort of radical shift in the way humans live is probably inevitable. That shift is likely to be toward what I have called "the shadows." The question then remaining is whether or not the shadows will be a sanctuary worth the wanting.

Chapter 4

Denial's Undeniable Pleasures

I will not go into great detail in this small book with statistical evidence now at hand, and frequently recited, about world-wide environmental degradation. That evidence has now become a veritable mountain of data available in any good library. There are fine works that are forty or more years old, such as the two-volume *Man's Role in Changing the Face of Nature*, edited by William Thomas, as well as many current studies such as papers in *State of the World* volumes put out each year by The Worldwatch Institute. Most such works have lengthy bibliographies of biological and economic reports, which have, in turn, extensive statistical research citations of their own.

The great irony of the mountain of evidence documenting world-wide environmental deterioration is that the bigger and more obvious the mountain grows the more intense the psychological denial and displacement responses it sets in motion.

This is what happened, for instance, when the *Global 2000* report, a multi-volume publication, was issued by the Carter administration in 1980. It contained not only a lot of basic factual information but also some fairly depressing interpretations of what it implied.

Herman Kahn and Julian Simon immediately produced a rosier interpretation of things, called *Global 2000 Revised*. The Kahn-Simon piece contains such wondrous statements as, "If present trends continue, the world in 2000 will be less crowded, less polluted, more stable ecologically, and less vulnerable than the world we live in now." And then they go themselves one better, raising living-in-denial to the level of an art form. Deforestation rates are "not worrisome" and "there is no evidence for the rapid loss of species."

Back in 1968 biologist Paul Erlich published his best-selling *Population Bomb*. He was immediately hooted down by critics such as Kahn who pointed out that the bomb had not yet gone off in the industrial world's face. Which is also why "growth" advocates behaved as if they had been scalded when Dennis and Donalla Meadows published *The Limits to Growth* in 1972. The Meadows' computer analyses of human populations and nonrenewable resources implied that there were, like it or not, limits to how many people the earth can support. It too was hooted down because the industrial world did not collapse the day after the book came out.

Kahn, at the Hudson Institute, was one of those affronted by *The Limits to Growth*. In his *The Next Two Hundred Years*, a 1976 paean to the wonders of modern technology, he said that the Meadows had raised "false, nonexistent" issues. And with remarkable hubris he announced that within two hundred years people "almost everywhere" will be "numerous, rich and in control of nature."

It was one of the more fatuous observations from the futurist community. Chernobyl had not yet exploded when Kahn made his grandiose predictions. He had not known of the disasters in the fall-out regions of Chernobyl. He did not know that the *New York Times* would tell us in April of 1995, that in Japan, China and Taiwan alone, a hundred and fifteen commercial and research reactors were in operation and that the International Atomic Energy Agency would predict that power demands in

Asia would triple by the year 2015, that is, twenty years. The problem of living with the radioactive waste from so many reactors beggars the imagination. Hardly a world "rich and in control of nature."

Kahn did not know that ferocious debates would break out over the possible explosion of nuclear waste dumps in Yucca Mountain, Nevada, and that, as *Science* put it in June of 1995, "The cost of the [atomic waste burial] project has been prodigious--$1.7 billion and climbing fast." Charles Fosberg, head of a group at Oak Ridge studying the problem, in a stunning understatement, called disposal of 400,000 tons of depleted uranium left over from the arms race a "non-trivial problem." The problem is how to store canisters of waste safely for "at least 10,000 years," which is to say, 10,800 years longer than Kahn's two hundred years of ardent prosperity.

And now, daily stories appear in the media about millions of refugees and "illegals" moving restlessly, often desperately, across national boundaries all over the planet, in Southeast Asia, Africa, Europe, the Americas, armies of people on the move, trying to find enough to eat and a place to sleep. Numerous, to be sure, but hardly rich and in control of nature.

The sort of denial thinking that Kahn represents never really goes away, despite the evidence. In 1995 Gregg Easterbrook wrote *A Moment on the Earth*, subtitled "The Coming Age of Environmental Optimism." He talks, for instance, about the end of ocean dumping of raw sewage in 1992 in a few areas of the world, as if it was some sort of great leap forward. But he does not seriously consider the pollution of entire river systems around the world as the result of accelerating deforestation. And he talks of the need to eliminate water-borne diseases of children, without serious consideration of the spurt in population that occurs whenever we intervene significantly to lessen the impact of such diseases. One can only conclude that while women may come from Venus and men may come from Mars, to paraphrase the title of a recent bestseller, Easterbrook appears to have come from a feelgood planet yet to be discovered.

And then there is Francis Fukuyama's 1992 book *The End of History and the Last Man.* It drew a lot of attention and is interesting to read. It makes the usual arguments against twentieth century "pessimism" and presents the usual case for world-wide privatization of economies. He argues that the nineteenth century as contrasted with the twentieth century had a lot more going for it from an optimist's point of view. It was a time, he says, when "Nature, long man's adversary, would be mastered by modern technology and made to serve the end of human happiness." And Fukuyama provides us a list of "liberal democracies' that includes, strange to be sure, such places as the Dominican Republic, Singapore and Lebanon. He says these "free and democratic" forms of government will continue to spread because of "discoveries about the nature of man, whose truth does not diminish but grows more evident as one's point of view becomes more cosmopolitan." (Shades of William Godwin during one of his more giddy moments back in the 1790s.)

Of course, nature has never been "man's adversary" except in his own myopic view. In fact, were we able to ask Nature what it thinks of our "mastery" it would undoubtedly suggest it does very well without it. It would probably tell us to stop snapping our suspenders and go away. For instance, the cattle we coop up in cages as calves, so that their meat remains tender, would probably decline further mastery. And hogs whose noses we break so that they do not damage each other living in congested cells would probably say the same thing. As for wild Nature, there are too many species being driven to extinction for the rest of them to appreciate the delights of human mastery.

What Fukuyama construes as the "end of history" is a play on Hegelian dialectics, itself species-centric double talk, just as was its spawn, Marxism. The "triumph of liberal democracy" Fukuyama speaks of is the triumph of free-enterprise. But the word "free" in "free-enterprise" means what it says. It means the freedom to use resources pell-mell with little thought of tomorrow. Which is all well and good as long as tomorrow never comes.

The "triumph of liberal democracy" and "free enterprise" is really, if we may borrow again from biological thought, a "bloom-phase" in human domination of the planet, not unlike the "bloom phase" of other species rampantly exploiting their nutrients as long as they last. In our case the nutrients are mostly petroleum, gas, coal, fresh water, top soil and what grows on it.

But we should not forget that communism in the Soviet Union and National Socialism in Germany were brought to grief to a great extent by out-of-control development creeds. Stalin unleased every sort of preposterous five-year plan to "conquer nature." So did Adolph Hitler's National Socialism. And their collapse does not mean that the same natural laws that applied to their state capitalist deformities do not apply to us. And when Khrushchev boasted that his economy would "bury" ours, he was talking the same way that any swashbuckling Western industrial C.E.O. might talk to a rival over a second vodka on the rocks.

We do not like to look the matter in the eye, of course, but the fact is that freedom and material plenty cannot be maximized at the same time, unless we change what we mean by material plenty or rewrite the laws of nature. This explains, in part at least, why discontent around the world intensifies as resources play out. Wars over fresh water in the near east, for instance, are just over the horizon. In fact, the squabbling has already begun. When the meat is off the carcass, dogs fight the more ferociously over the bones.

The triumph of liberal democracy and free enterprise, Fukuyama suggests, could mean a quite boring future. With the great, heroic struggles of capitalism won, with the last dialectic spasm of conflict behind capitalism and communism over, we could find ourselves, as it were, in the locker room staring at each other, the season over, for good.

But I think there is good reason for a perverse kind of comfort on this point at least. Free-enterprise's hour of triumph seems a pyrrhic victory. It is already disturbed by the sounds of new cries and conflicts, and new enigmatic contests of non-reason. There are grisly struggles between war lords and messiahs, between cults, tribes and ethnicities. Secession movements are everywhere. Religious fundamentalism is colliding with bizarre new pagan displays of free-enterprise thinking. Consider Bob Briner's *The Management Methods of Jesus* or Laurie Beth Jones' *Jesus C.E.O.* (Salmon Rushdie's problems are probably only the beginning.) And then there are all those new forms of escape "coming on line," new street drugs, orgies on the Internet, even new talk of "conquering" the poor, helpless planet Mars.

And when Joel E. Cohen wrote a book in 1996 called *How Many People Can the Earth Support?*, a reviewer, an economist naturally enough, asked "if the earth is reaching carrying capacity because of land or food or energy shortages, where are the warning signs?" It is as if the reviewer had given up on newspapers, even second-rate newspapers, and had never heard of the "third world," which is most of the world, and had no idea at all of what carrying capacity really means in biology.

Similarly, when Lester Brown of the World Watch Institute, a very thoughtful person, published *Who Will Feed China?*, Vaclav Smil, a reviewer writing in the February 1996 issue of the *New York Review of Books*, took Brown to task for being a pessimist who saw trouble ahead for China. Smil goes on to make a case for the possible, short-run increase in grain and meat production in China. And he ridicules "pessimists" as the kind of people who said we were "running out of oil" during the OPEC crisis of 1974. We have been running out of oil, of course, ever since the first oil gusher came in.

Smil does not ask that hard, ineluctable question that everyone who makes predictions of his kind should ask, "And then what?" China's resources are not infinite, nor will it be spared rule by natural correctives any more than any other land. It is precisely because Chinese authorities are pessimistic about the future without radical birth control that they have initiated what is, in fact, a brutal, and only partially successful, effort to control population. Meanwhile the figure of Malthus hovers over the discussion of both optimists and pessimists. He refuses to go away.

But the present picture of the planet, from an environmental point of view, is bleak, like it or not. Take, for example, Robert

Kaplan's *The Ends of the Earth*, a 1996 book. I mentioned it earlier, in passing. It is a reporter's story from the field, immediate, and for the most part unflinching, in its forecasting. Kaplan visited West Africa, Egypt, Anatolia, Iran, India, Central Asia and South East Asia. His firsthand report on social disintegration, environmental degradation and the pathologies of uncontrolled population growth is unremittingly grim, with a few, small exceptions here and there, such as in the Rishi valley of south India. Kaplan repeats (but seems at times to shy away from) what many biologists have said for most of the twentieth century, that the ideas of Reverend Malthus cannot be wished away.

Most of us in the so-called developed nations prefer to ignore the obvious implications of reports such as Kaplan's. Economists, in particular, have great trouble facing neo-Malthusian realities. They prefer to talk of the possibility of endless economic growth, dismissing costs of irreversible soil loss, water pollution, forest destruction and such, as external to their calculations. And they talk constantly of "sustainable development," an obvious oxymoron. There is no such possibility for any modern economy over any long period of time, on this or any other planet. This is as true for the new world economy as it is for a county landfill of plastic rubbish.

I believe this is the reason why groups such as Worldwatch often find it necessary to sugarcoat bad news with what good news they can scrape together. So the *State of the World* reports, for instance, are subtitled "Progress Toward a Sustainable Society," even though the evidence of sustainability, baring very radical reductions in birthrates and standards of living in the developed world, is slim indeed. So even the best people in the environmental movement are forced to go along with the deceits of that blissful little band of development junkies who cannot bear to be serious about tomorrow.

Here is a case of interest in this give-and-take of changing values in a post-modernist world. *New York Times Magazine* writer John Tierney, in May 1996, with tongue in cheek perhaps, came up with the idea that we could make a space trip to Mars by turning the entire effort into a grand, promotional stunt, a new version, he says, of Amundsen's and Shakelton's expeditions to the Poles. Tierney proposed that we use every marketing gimmick we can come up with, "to make millions," even though it was believed at the time the proposal was published that there was nothing of intrinsic value that could justify going to Mars instead of spending the money on earth. He argued that the trip could be done more cheaply by the private sector than by NASA, which may well be true. But he insisted the project could be justified by market considerations here on earth, sales tie-ins, talk shows, sound bites, auctioning shoes that walked Mars, mountain-naming rights, toy sales and broadcasts "Live From the Red Planet." The proposal was justified by good old-fashioned entrepreneurship and the free-lunch theory of economics.

Tierney totally missed the point that going to Mars has intrinsic social costs, that it is inevitably a priority question. It does not have the political value of our moon trip, which was basically to one-up the Soviet Union. Of course, now that there is some evidence of fossil microbial forms on Mars, the whole matter of going back to the planet is again up in the air. *Science* magazine suggests that the discovery, if it holds up, will give NASA a new lease on life. The ball is presumably back in the court of public priorities. But, of course, that is where it has always been, privatized or not.[*]

Take another case from our everyday reading, the case of the Unabomber. In an April, 1996 opinion piece in *Newsweek*, Joe Klein writes about the Unabomber and his string of killings. Usually a thoughtful, sometimes witty (if ethically challenged), journalist, Klein goes careening off the topic of serial killing and Luddite hatred of technology into denunciation of Nature lovers. He seized on a line in the Unabomber's manifesto which says,

---

[*]The latest call to go to Mars, by former Martin Marietta engineer Robert Subrin and his co-author Richard Wagner is found in their 1996 book, *The Case for Mars: The Plan to Settle the Red Planet and Why We Must*, reviewed in December 1996 in the *New York Times Book Review*. Evidently we are to go to Mars to prove that we are "still a nation of pioneers" and unintimidated by "Malthusianism."

"The positive ideal we propose is Nature." Klein scoffs, "You remember Nature. It was big before Marx." Then with the odd, misshapen logic of displacement, he attacks tree hugging: "The pursuit of the primitive--like hugging trees--comes when rich nations begin to indulge themselves."

Environmentalists and neo-Luddites, Klein suggests, have made a kind of mad prophet of the killer bomber. All this is said with an apparent straight face, even though something like 60% to 70% of the American public now calls itself environmentalist. The column is illustrated, of course, by four young people stripped to the waist and hugging trees.

Strange, to be sure, this claim that tree-hugging is the result of affluence. But what is stranger is that Klein seems unaware that tree-hugging is a very ancient practice. So is the metaphoric capitalization of Nature. The Christmas tree, after all, is a form of tree-hugging. It was, at least, before crude mall marketeering trashed Christmas. And Buddha received his spiritual insights sitting under a tree. Whether he hugged it or not I am not sure. I would guess he did now and again. And there is a sacred olive tree on the Acropolis, if pollution has not killed it by now. Indeed, St. Francis' retreat at Eremo Delle Carceri has a 1,000-year-old oak under which he is said to have meditated. And Saint Clare liked to describe herself as "the little plant of Blessed Francis."

There is no particular mystery about why people hug trees and capitalize Nature. It has nothing to do with affluence. The human species evolved within a natural world and regard for nature was the same as regard for survival. Which is why primitive hunters often offered prayers of thanks to an animal they killed to eat or skin. The dinner table prayer many of us grew up with, "Blessed Our Lord for these thy gifts ..." is the same kind of ecological response.

This does not mean that primitive man is necessarily wise, or that "pursuing the primitive" is necessarily wise. It only means that some habits pay off better than others, again, in the long run. The fact is that prehistoric hunters were sometimes as stupid as any modern-day industrial polluter. They evidently brought about the extinction of some species of megafauna they used for food, hides and bone-strut shelter without realizing that they were doing so. And it was not unusual, we might add, for some North American Plains Indians to stampede entire herds of buffalo over cliffs to get what they wanted in meat and hides. This was hardly an ecologically sensitive approach to their problems, unless there were millions of buffalo and a lot fewer Indians.

But when we see a New Guinea tribesman on documentary television screaming his rage at Japanese paper pulp companies in the act of clear cutting his forested homeland, that scream being, "You are tearing the skin from our mother earth!" it means that the tribesman is instinctively reacting to ecological threat, and the scream makes perfectly good sense as a type of tree-hugging. But imbedded in that scream is an ecological regulator trying to make a difference. The scream has the same function that joining the Wilderness Society or the Audubon Society ought to have.

So "Nature" was, indeed, "big before Marx." In fact, one of the more horrible features of communism, which is often called "state capitalism" for very good reason, is its disdain for Nature, not to mention Marx's disdain for Reverend Malthus' ideas on population. In fact, Stalin's megalomanic schemes for conquering nature, his plans to reverse the flow of several Arctic rivers, for instance, puts him well up among the great "land developers" of our times. So were his engineers and their ecologically purblind plans to use water from the Aral Sea to increase cotton production in Uzbekistan, an absolute disaster as it turned out.

This sort of thing, as well as crimes committed against the planet by atomic testing and pollution, are the topics of the book by Murray Feshbach and Alfred Friendly, Jr., called *Ecocide in the USSR*. Ironically, Friendly was bureau chief in Moscow for *Newsweek*, the magazine that runs Klein's columns. But we must remind ourselves that communist outrages against "Nature" are no dumber in principle than American dams that destroy salmon fisheries while they pipe electric power to cities intent on looking like Las Vegas. Nor are they any more absurd in principle than establishment of such communities as Sun City, Arizona.

So I think it is fair to say that tree-hugging is a great deal more than a smug put-down phrase invented by a philistine with a chain saw. Denouncing technology's arrogant ways and capitalizing Nature does not make the Unabomber or some angry Luddite a misguided Francis of Assisi. And certainly talking to birds, being charitable (especially if one comes, as did Francis, from a wealthy family) and writing Canticles to the Sun is a more effective way of gaining followers than blowing up strangers with mail bombs. Unfortunately, however, most of us, and Joe Klein, do not want to face the possibility that someone can be mad and prophetic at the same time. In fact, if someone is a symptom of trouble in his or her times, no matter how goofy, murderous or unwitting, the symptom remains prophetic.

All of this will bring to mind again the fate of any "pessimistic" interpretation of what the future holds as the world degrades ecologically. But, as Tom Athanasiou suggests in *Divided Planet: The Ecology of Rich and Poor*, ecologically speaking, "Optimism is a greater danger than apocalyptic fear." It is dangerous not only because it allows us to deceive ourselves but also because it provides cover for those industrial interests who mask their squalid ways by putting a phony ecological spin on their advertising.

To be sure, pessimism is less than a prepossessing philosophy of life and hardly an outlook most people study to achieve. Schoepenhauer was probably the greatest systematic pessimist thinker, though some have said he would have been less disposed to proving that unsatisfied "Will" was the root of our miseries had his mother not thrown him down the stairs early in life. But from a strict cybernetic, or automatic control, point of view, pessimism can often serve usefully as a standard against which our actual chances are played out. It is an operation of the past in dealing with the present. As I suggested earlier, that was one of the vital functions of "original sin."

And when we look at nature, even casually, it is hard not to conclude that there is a good deal of pessimism built into things.

Witness the shell of a turtle or the protective coloration of an insect. Building castles and fortifications is also all about pessimism. And humans have spent an inordinate amount of time at such sweaty work. To be sure, we may not want to "live in fear," as the phrase goes, but one can easily imagine that a goodly dose of pessimism early on about what people like Adolph Hitler were up to could have spared us a lot of pain.

The phrase "fool's paradise" did not appear in our lexicon by accident. It appears to have earned its keep. That is why from an ecological point of view all of the up-beat talk about risk taking that we hear now in commercial quarters has such a suspicious ring. The only good reason for taking a risk in a really serious matter (which is why we prefer to do it in games) is because we have to. So when we hear, "Do not take counsel from thy fears!" we should remember that our fears are sometimes the best counsel of all.

For some writers these many problems, frustrations and plain failure to control environmental deterioration have triggered a kind of wishful "back to the genetic drawing board" response. In his review of Philip Shabecoff's 1996 *A New Name For Peace* and Tom Athanasious' *Divided Planet*, Mark Dowie quotes Shabecoff as saying, "Homo sapiens will have to find some way to bid farewell to its evolutionary childhood."

Unfortunately a million years of evolution has anchored our "childhood" in our genes. Barring some incredible global retooling of human genetics, which would make global birth-control seem easy by comparison, "human nature" is not going to change.

But the fact that neo-Malthusian principles are here to stay, in the face of all sorts of denial, is evident in the recent writing of historians of the caliber of Paul Kennedy. He was author of *The Rise and Fall of the Great Powers*, a book well received several years ago. His more recent book, however, *Preparing for the Twenty-First Century*, which came out in 1994, discusses Malthusian ideas at length, population growth, resource depletion and such. He concludes, for instance, that "What is clear is that as the Cold War fades away, we face not a 'new world order' but a troubled and fractured planet ...." And he speaks of the need for politicians and publics to come to grips with demographic realities. And in a sad, last-hope sort of way, he says that even Malthus "was at least willing to admit that *theoretically* [emphasis Kennedy's] humankind could change its ways and avoid the fate predicted for it."

It would be well, to be sure, if humankind could change its ways. Most of us wish we could. We feel better when we think we can. But in a strange, convoluted way all of these developments, neo-Malthusian announcements, and pronounce-ments, and their denial, or the displacement of our anxieties about the future of the "developed world," in which we scapegoat anybody or anything handy, are all, if I may beat the poor phrase almost to death, "post-modern." But the critical feature of post-modernism is not simply some new dismembering habit in literature, or something new in painting or architecture. *The key feature of "post-modernism" is the return to the Western psyche of the sense of limitation.* This sense of limitation is the very antithesis of the grand myths of progress and human perfectibility that were the foundation of modernism.

The mutinous murmur across the "less developed countries," the LDCs, toward the selfishness and greed of the "developed world" with its endless boasts of endless "development" possibilities, is itself a post-modern phenomenon. So too is the curious effort to cure poverty in the LDCs with tourism. It does not change the relationship of rich tourists to poverty-stricken flunkies. It only moves the relationship from one port of call to another. Strange though it may sound, those enormous pleasure cruise ships that now ply the oceans and keep affluent tourists safe from third-world muggers are themselves post-modern phenomena.

Oddly enough so too is the fanciful conviction that the faster "information" flies about the planet by computers, the more secure we will all be. Even the strange euphemisms we use now to replace the tired old term "progress" have an odd post-modern quality, the way the word "growth!" is now tossed about as some sort of new panacea, or the call for "change!," as if "change" was always for the better. And if none of this is sufficient to ease our anxiety we can always go out and buy a book for easy reading at the beach, even though we may have to ignore the pollution warning signs at the water's edge.

We ought to be very skeptical of anyone who pits optimism against realism, or pessimism against the joys of a spring day in May. But if there is evidence that pleasant spring days are becoming fewer, it is time to surrender some of the optimism to pessimism's cold steel.

So once again we are back struggling with Reason's claims, as in the days of Condorcet and Godwin, and fearful of the cost of the elegant amnesia that goes with sustaining our faith in it. This should not mean that we have to forget if we are to dream. But beneath all the wishes loom two grim twenty-first century realities, a probable world-wide population explosion and the ecological disaster that would go with it. They are as powerful in their way as the collision of continental plates.

Chapter 5

Time, Place and Ego

The high optimism of the eighteenth century had opened the door to all sorts of ambitious schemes for the redesign of human nature itself. If man was naturally good and naturally rational, it followed that society ought to be arranged to allow him his best shot at the stars. Claude Helvetius was one such thinker. Another of that doughty little band working on the twenty-eight volume Encyclopedie under Denis Diderot's editorship, he not only believed all men more-or-less equally endowed, but he also saw "indefinite malleability" in human nature. He also foresaw a "science of morals equivalent to the science of legislation." He was cut, suggest Bury and Becker, from the same cloth as social engineers such as Claude Saint-Simon, whose writings foreshadow European socialist thought and the work of Auguste Comte, inventor of the term "sociology."

Comte saw himself as a scientist, but he also thought the result of untended human freedom could be "intellectual anarchy," and he concluded that a priest-like caste of sociologists were needed to keep things straight. Down to the present day many sociologists think of themselves in that role, though all too often they show up in classrooms in jeans rather than priestly robes, child-like "first learners" in the spent progressive education tradition.

From these efforts to make the study of history a science such figures as Karl Marx, Oswald Spengler, Arnold Toynbee and A. L. Kroeber emerge, each searching for a pattern to history and, finding it. Marxism was especially proud of its scientific pretensions. Kroeber, an anthropologist, on the other hand, published his *Configurations of Culture Growth* in 1944 and is one of the more interesting illustrations of history become social science. He conducted detailed comparative studies of growth patterns in literature, art, science, drama and music in Europe, China, Japan, India and the Muslim worlds. It was an impressive achievement, rather along the lines of Oswald Spengler's 1926 and 1928 two-volume work, *The Decline of the West*, and to which Kroeber tips his hat.

As a new sociological virtuosity came on the scene, the study of history, at least a good part of it, was evolving into the study of progress systematics. It was not a matter of trying to forget or disown history as some men of the Enlightenment wanted to do, or simply a matter of trying to be rational about it. The longitudinal axis of attention was being turned on its side and the present, the moment, became the focal point. In the middle of the moment, of course, is the ego.*

These developments had corollaries in psychology and sociology. In 1951 Kurt Lewin's *Field Theory in Social Science* appeared, one of many such books attempting to define a "field at a given time," "life spaces" and "valances," the latter term until then largely associated with chemistry. Lewin's book is

---

*Part of the reason for this shift in perspective was that anthropologists, particularly British ethnologists, found themselves in colonial situations studying people who did not have writing, no "history" in the usual sense. So a kind of snapshot view of culture appeared in the form of functionalism. To this day, the nature of the "ethnographic present" is a point of debate in archeological studies of buried "history." The "history" of any people is, of course, encoded in its customs and traditions. The destruction of custom or tradition amounts to loss by a people of its memory of its past.

replete with mathematical definitions of every sort, attempts to apply "hard science" analysis to group dynamics. During this time small group analysis and "sociometry," a term invented by J. L. Moreno, also came on the scene with efforts to measure the push and pull of social choice and rejection. One-way-glassed laboratories appeared in which the interaction of children as well as adults could be studied. Many of these studies were laced with good, if naive, efforts to get at the roots of authoritarian, as against democratic, ways of behaving. But, of course, the idea of progress still drove many of these studies. Lewin's first chapter, for instance, is titled "Formalization and Progress in Psychology."

Parallel to what was going on in the sciences, a host of "isms" begin to show up, some in politics, some in the arts, some in both, but all with a chip on their shoulder toward history and tradition. Futurism, cubism, suprematism, minimalism, even conceptualism, were driven by the romance of change, in one form or the other, the idea of progress. One of the more notorious "isms" was Italian futurism, founded by Fillippo Marinetti and launched with his famous manifesto from Milan in 1909:

> ... a manifesto of sweeping, incendiary violence with which we found Futurism. We want to liberate this country of its fetid gangrene of professors, archaeologists [presumably because they were forever digging up the 'past'], Latinists, and antique dealers.

Futurism, he said, required nothing less than "the complete renovation of the human psyche."

This was not, as I said, the first or last time we would hear a call for the making of a new kind of man. It happened with the French Revolution, with socialism and communism, with virtually every "ism" in the arts that came along, such as work at the Bauhaus and even, of course, with Frank Lloyd Wright's demand for wholesale rethinking of what architecture was to be.

Wright spells it out well in nine, very blunt rules in his essay *Prairie Architecture*, in 1910. But like most leaders in the arts of his time, Wright was spellbound by the machine. His was, after all, the age of Amelia Earhart and Charles Lindbergh. In another of his essays Wright declares,"That the Machine has dealt Art in the grand old sense a death-blow, none will deny." And considering the profound impact that the camera, as a machine, especially the motion picture camera, had on art, few could deny that he was correct.

Since Wright's time, or the work of great modernists like Walter Gropius or Mies Van der Rohe, post-modernists have overrun a substantial piece of the architectural terrain, even though they have seldom been able to build work on the captured ground that rivals the disciplined grandeur of the best of the modernists.

That is why, in my view, the writing of such post-modernist architects as Michael Graves is more about metaphor and mood than it is about the story of how modernism got to be post-modernism. In his 1983 essay, "A Case For Figurative Architecture," he argues that the "metaphor of the machine" has lost its grip and that architectural language should express "the mythic and ritual aspirations of society."

Graves' argument is notable, I think, for several reasons in particular. One is that societies do not really "aspire" to myth and ritual. Myth and ritual cannot be wished into existence. They coalesce from non-rational social forces around them. They cannot simply be invented without running the risk of having them used as Dr. Goebbels used the ancient swastika. Myth and ritual are cultural concatenations "in the shadows."

There is something else about Graves' point of view that deserves attention. It is that it exposes the vulnerability of the machine metaphor in a post-Hiroshima world. And it implies that a great deal of non-conscious search, or scanning (in the cybernetic sense) is taking place in the aesthetics of our time.

Yet Graves' plea for myth and ritual is, at heart I believe, a plea to back away from the claims of rationalist optimism, a sort of back-handed way of acknowledging the principle of limitation. For it is notable that the appeal for myth and ritual is a quasi-religious appeal. Henri Bergson told us back in 1932 that religion has a reassembling effect on meaning in our lives. The myth-making function of religion, he says, has "consolidation of society" as its "first function." It puts together the shards and fragments left us by the "dissolvent" powers of reason.

What Graves seems to be asking for is the sort of idealized memories that Kotre referred to, and which I cited earlier. Seen through Bergson's eyes, Graves' argument becomes a religious argument. And while religion helps us put things together, in the process it sets limits on what does and does not belong.

It is interesting to add, too, that Francis Fukuyama's book, *The End of History*, which came out in 1992, is often called another case of an "ism," in this case a sort of final triumphant wave from the top rung of the ladder of capitalism. And even as the champions of laissez-faire economics stand victorious on the rubble heap of communism, they envision the twenty-first century as a great, fast-forward consumerist Eden.

To be sure, progressivism has always informed the free-enterprise world, both during and after the industrial revolution. The world was seen as a market, always a bigger and more boisterous market. True, we in the United States have removed filth-belching smokestacks from our postage stamps. But we have not given up our grand plans, not willingly at least. For instance, we intend to map the genetic world from end to end and "push the envelope," as we like to say, of biological engineering right into the murky, ethical realm of redesigning babies. And now, having "conquered" the moon, and having left our litter on it, we draw up grand plans for populating unsuspecting planets.

Now that we have found evidence of microscopic life on Mars it will be interesting to see what we try to do about it. Will it send Copernican shock waves through the fundamentalist religious community? Will it go largely ignored? Will some bright, young biologist try to copy these primitive forms and then colonize an ocean just to see if the results are "interesting?" And once again we end up where we began, struggling with Pascal's principle of limits.

Even such brilliant, modern philosophic minds as Ludwig Wittgenstein, as spectacular an intellect as any in recent times, was caught in the forked stick of self-limiting rationality. At one point in his famous 1919 *Tractatus Logico-Philosophicus* he announces that "Everything that can be said can be said clearly." Which was taken by many logical-empiricists, especially of the Vienna Circle, to mean that all science, ultimately all knowledge therefore, can be reduced to the languages of physics and mathematics. And, of course, they loathed metaphysics as the last stronghold of fuzzy mindedness. But Wittgenstein ends his tract with one of the grand, oracular statements of modern thought, "Whereof we cannot speak, thereof we must be silent." Which means that most of life and love, most of its mirth, and grieving, and its expressions in music, ritual, dance, theater, poetry and painting, lie in the shadows, beyond the reach of reason.

Let me summarize for convenience's sake some of the ideas I presented in these last chapters. One idea is that concepts such as "original sin" and "wisdom of the ancients" had social cybernetic uses. They represent what cyberneticists call a "reference signal," a standard or model, against which "real" behavior is to be measured, and by which error is calculated.

Set points, or reference signals, do not exist merely because we like them, or the way they may lay on the pages of scripture. They act like giant flywheels of belief and they help maintain, if they work reasonably well, a degree of equilibrium. They help damp aberrant behavior, or yawing, and minimize the need for abrupt change. They help to make things move slowly, or appear to. Which is why, for instance, many Westerners, both before and after the Renaissance, took the view that since the great days of Greece and Rome, things were never quite as glorious. Greece and Rome had become models in the Western mind. Their gruesome features, such as slavery and love of gore, had been pared away in the making of a mythic stereotype that could then function as a reference signal, and figures such as Pericles,

Solon and Cicero could do their duty as heroes for generations to come.

But borrowing from Norbert Wiener, the inventor of the term "cybernetics," in his book of that title published in 1948, we "predict the future of a curve [any pattern in fact] by carrying out a certain [mathematical] operation on its past." Which is a basic probability principle, a way of saying that if a thing repeats itself repeatedly it is more likely to repeat itself again. Carrying out a "certain operation on the past" means that we make predictions, against some sort of set-point, like any ordinary thermostat does. That is why, as I suggested, cultures are inherently conservative, and why too if they remain too conservative in the face of change, the "task environment" as it is often called, they are vulnerable.

We can highlight the point by citing the evolutionary principle known as "Romer's Rule." A. S. Romer was a paleontologist. Two writers, Charles Hockett and Robert Ascher, phrase Romer's Rule this way, in a 1969 book of ecological readings, edited by Paul Shepard and Daniel McKinley, called *The Subversive Science*:

> The initial survival value of a favorable innovation is conservative, in that it renders possible the maintenance of a traditional way of life in the face of changed circumstances. Later on, of course, the innovation may allow the exploration of some ecological niche not available to the species before the change; but this is a consequence, not a cause.

One of the species Romer studied was the lungfish.

"Man is not a lungfish!" one can almost hear Diderot, or a real estate developer, shout. But Romer's point is that nature is not purposely good, not struggling toward some higher order of being, but simply trying to keep one foot in front of the other. The creatures of the sea did not leave the sea because they wished to become land animals. They left the sea because many found themselves in tidal areas in which life on land culled out those that could not survive outside water on a full-time basis. It was one small incremental adaptation after another. And humans did not strive to leave the cave because they dreamed of living in suburbia. They left the cave because they were hungry, or the climate changed, or the roof caved in. And so natural systems, including cultures, as Romer's Rule suggests, are inherently conservative. But this should give small comfort to political conservatives still wedded to the great, grand myths of endless "development" and "progress," for those ideas are the precise antithesis of what Romer was talking about. Romer's Rule is as true for us as for the lungfish.

In fact, the lungfish may have the advantage. Living much of the time in the mud, it would be difficult for the creature to become a narcissist. Not so with modern, or even post-modern man. He has wrecked the gyroscope of tradition and thrown the flywheel of past experience out the window. He grins, like Narcissus, down into the pool of his ego. He sees no evil leaven. More often than not he rather likes what he sees, or tries hard to convince himself that he does.

Chapter 6

I Feel, Therefore I Am Afraid

The optimism of the philosophers of the eighteenth and early nineteenth centuries did not derive merely from their pleasure in kicking over the theological traces of the Church, nor from watching the flywheel of ancient, traditional beliefs disintegrate. It derived as well from a radical foreshortening of historical perspective. In my opinion, this is but another evidence of the paradigm shift I spoke of earlier.

Let me cite a quotation about the arts from Ortega y Gasset. It goes straight at the issue. It is an insight that applies far beyond the arts.

> The guiding law of the great variations in [Western] painting is one of disturbing simplicity. First things are painted; then sensations; finally ideas. ... These three stages are three points on a straight line.

Ortega had identified a fundamental shift in the way the West construes reality, less and less a thing "out there" beyond the individual, less and less something like Emmanuel Kant's "phenomena," or a "neumena" lurking behind it, more and more skin-contained sensations, feelings of the individual. But this new reality is also a solipsistic dead-end.

One of the more dazzling displays of our confrontation with that dead-end was existentialist philosophy. For sheer brilliance some of the existential thinkers have few rivals, Soren Kierkegaard, for instance, who lived from 1813 to 1855, or Miguel Unamuno, living from 1864 to 1936, or Friedrich Nietzsche, who lived from 1844 to 1900, and Albert Camus who lived from 1914 to 1960. But often existentialism became a hyper-rational attempt to turn the flanks of feeling. Jean Paul Sartre, 1905-1980, comes to mind. And then there were all sorts of parade ground displays of self-deception by deconstructionists, a kind of halting wanna-be latter-day existentialism, a movement that took strange delight in dismembered reasoning, and possessed a morbid fear of common sense.

But each was in its own way a form of hyper-rationalism, an effort to think through what we know through our pores, all those strange compelling private and collective needs, habits of love and hate toward the gods, mysterious urges to participate in rite and ritual, to hold fast to myths, to recite epic tribal poetry by light of campfire, to make art and to dance, to mark our presence on cliff walls with petroglyphs, to savor the meat and bread of anger and forgiveness, following whatever it is that causes Australian aborigines to dance, the Ainu to pray over a bear they have killed, or New Age cults to find magic in pyramids and crystals.

The subjectivist predicament of the Western mind is especially obvious in the romantic arts. Take the case of Walter Pater. He dates from 1839 to 1894. A new biography of Pater by Denis Donoghue is full of examples of what I mean. Consider Pater's famous lines, "To burn with this hard, gem-like flame, to maintain this ecstasy, is success in life. Failure is to form habits; for habit is relative to a stereotype."

From an anthropological point of view at least, Pater has it all backwards. Cultures, societies, preexist the individual. It is not the other way around. And cultures, societies, are systems of habit. To build systems of habit we categorize, classify and package personal experience into generalizations, into stereotypes. That some stereotypes, some generalizations, can be false, misleading or venal, does not mean that we must not stereotype daily experience, assembling the blizzard of events around us into categories. Categories make prediction possible.

Jerome Bruner, the eminent psychologist, argued in a classic paper called "On Perceptual Readiness," in 1957, that "perception involves an act of categorization," and that "If perceptual experience is ever had raw, i.e., free of categorical identity, it is doomed to be a gem serene, locked in the silence of private experience."

Cultures, societies, are, after all, complex structures of roles and rules. They make it possible to speak of "the butcher," "the baker" and the "candlestick maker," of "fathers," "mothers," "brothers" and "uncles." We regularly process our daily experience by such prefabricated classifications, classifications handed down to us from the past. Were this not possible we would have to treat every experience as if it were unique. The world would dissolve into an unpredictable buzz that makes no sense. Comparison would be impossible.

Milan Kundera, the novelist, in one of his essays, *You're Not in Your Own House Here, My Dear Fellow*, touches on an interesting facet of the tendency to confuse the public and private sides of life. He puts the problem this way:

> An old revolutionary utopia, whether fascist or communist: life without secrets where public life and private life are one and the same. The surrealist dream Andre Breton loved: the glass house ... Ah, the beauty of transparency! The only successful realization of this dream: a society totally monitored by the police.

The confusion in our time over the difference between public and private is related in a special way to what Ortega observed. That is why extreme subjectivism, Pater's reality, carries the cost that it does, the hazard of having one's personal reality put to perverse use. To begin with it isolates the individual in a transparent, subjective bubble where the individual simultaneously displays himself, or herself, while laying claim to the singleness of an experience. But the bubble is transparent. Images are distorted looking into as well as looking out of it.

We live today in what Peter Kramer, author of *Listening to Prozac*, calls an "era of autopathography," in which "bookshelves groan with memoirs of heart disease and asthma. No mental disorder, from alcoholism and autism to schizophrenia, is without its confession."

He believes autopathography "reflects a cultural commitment to diversity, a welcome, oddly joyous sign of tolerance." But he wonders "just how far social utility carries any genre." And it is important to add that with the case of alcoholism it is precisely the anonymous, in Alcoholics Anonymous, that accounts for much of its remarkable success. So we face the larger question, What of the talk show culture in which millions of people immerse themselves daily in public display of the rancid side of private life? Is it simply electronically amplified Freudianism, cheapened to taste?

And hot off the press, in a *New York Times Magazine* May 1996 paper called Confessing for Voyeurs: The Age of the Literary Memoir is Now, James Atlas gives us twelve authors, each with a brief tell-all selection of memories. (The significance of "Now" in the title should not be missed.) Some of the authors give us brilliant, gripping accounts of this or that event that deeply affected their lives. But the new memoir literature, Atlas says, is a "virtual library of dysfunctional revelation." And he notes in his lead essay the case of a Princeton professor who reveals his sex relations with his dog, and another prominent writer recounting how he brought a woman to orgasm in the back seat of a car while his unsuspecting wife sat up-front.

William Gass' satirical observations about the narcissism of it all is included in the Atlas essay. "Look, Ma, I'm breathing. See me take my initial toddle, use the potty, scratch my sister, win spin the bottle. Gee Whiz, my first adultery--what a guy!"

We should add that this appears to be more confirmation of Ortega's law for western subjectivization and takes place in both the visual arts as well as in literature. The subject is no longer "out there," beyond the individual, but drawn steadily toward and into the self. From the realist masterworks of the Renaissance (even if the subjects were "real" angels) to the painting of such masters as Rembrandt or Hals, to impressionists like Monet, to dream-state surrealists like Dali, to the abstract expressionists like DeKooning and action painters like Pollock, to conceptualists like Kosuth and performance artists like Chris Burden (Burden had himself photographed as he was being shot by a bullet in the arm), the line is one of "disturbing simplicity," as Ortega says.

As we look back on it this whole business represents a basic paradigmatic shift in what Western mankind thinks himself to be. Where we go from here is just about anyone's guess. My guess is that this aesthetic line of development (or decay if one so chooses to call it) will break into all kinds of strands and tangles, some highly local, some ethnic, some "spacey" in a quite literal sense. This aesthetic chaos could be, of course, an invitation to new imposed versions of reality, instant traditions of the kind Hitler, Mao and Stalin imposed. It is very improbable that it will be some new, free expression of liberal democracy, some sort of "end of aesthetic history." We are already sunk to the armpits in that rich, new, free sort of thing and it has grown stale and wearisome to the eye as well as to the spirit.

But we should note that Pater's sort of truth, indeed all the self-caressing excesses of extreme romanticism, is not something entirely new. Many mystics have been given to the same thing, including the love of public display of their privacy. Saint Simeon Stylites, living for years on top a pillar, is an example. Apart from considerations of toilet, there is always a socially unfinished quality to their claims of truth. Which may account for why we like to call such people half-baked.

In any case, contrary to the "I think, therefore I am" claim of Descartes, feeling, not thought, is the primal resource in our experience, and it is a slippery thing. While it is possible to know thought and habit through feeling, it is not possible to feel a feeling authentically, second hand, by merely thinking about it. We do not use reason to apprehend feeling, but the other way around. Nor can we experience a cultural system of habits by merely thinking about them. Such habits are non-conscious rules for management of collectively experienced feeling. That is why it is notoriously difficult for an anthropologist really to understand another culture until he or she has lived in it for a long time, and sunk himself, or herself, in its group-held feelings.

Relocating the locus of meaning from society into the individual does not lessen the need for that "entire constellation of beliefs, values, techniques ... shared by members of a given community" to which Kuhn applied the word "paradigm." It merely exposes the individual to unsustainable demands of romantic isolation. It imprisons the individual in the obsessions that racked the existentialists.

Unamunos' great work *The Tragic Sense of Life* is as good an illustration as any. Brilliant, tormented, it represents a desperate effort of the author to free himself, naked and alone, from the pain of consciousness and realization of mortality. But it is a doomed effort, by its very nature tragic, a kind of solitary, unseen crucifixion. Instead of "I think, therefore I am," the proof of being becomes "I feel, therefore I am afraid!"

But to return to the Pater sort of solipsism. Oscar Wilde is perhaps as striking an illustration of life lived on those terms as any we know. He lived from 1854 to 1900 and is buried in the famed Lachaise Cemetery in Paris, his tomb, even now, sprayed with admiring graffiti, "We still love you Oscar!"

Brilliant, often dazzling, Wilde told the court sitting in judgment on charges of sodomy made against him in 1895, that perfect truth would be "something so personal that the same truth could never be appreciated by two minds." This takes Ortega's three stage course of subjectivization, indeed the very idea of truth, to the end of the line. With it the romanticist has sealed himself in an echo chamber, like a performance artist without an audience. The end stage becomes self as total "I," solitary, obsessive, final, entombed with the sound of its own making.

Consider the strange, solipsistic quality of a 1995 article in *The New York Times*, called "*Obscenity: A Celebration.*" It is a centennial two-page essay about Wilde, by Wayne Koestenbaum. It illustrates that curious confusion between what is public and what is private, that desperate love of transparency that the ego displays when it cannot know itself, that odd affliction to which Kundera refers. Koestenbaum hails Wilde as "a prophet of an impulse," someone who taught us "the value of the individual's desire, even to the point of anarchy." He hails Wilde as "perversity's finest diplomat" and says that "of his career's many acts the most beautiful was his disgrace." This is like saying deception's merits lie in the promise of self-deception.

The interesting thing about this sort of total surrender to privation of habit is not just that it generates the individual doubt that Peirce wrote about. It forces the individual more and more, if I may use Carl Jung's felicitous phrase, to "resort to decisions," without help from the experience of others, without that "ancestral help" I mentioned earlier, citing John Kotre. And, of course, the hallmark of the true romantic is his or her feigned rejection of such help in any form.

When we think of romanticism we commonly think of Jean Jacque Rousseau, especially his *Confessions*, in which he tells how he sometimes found himself sitting on a boulder on the shores of Lake Geneva watching his tears form circles in the water at his feet. Rousseau was a special kind of romantic, insofar as he thought of primitive man as living in a state of nature more idyllic than modern man. But there are other great romantics of this sort who as easily come to mind. There is François Chateaubriand writing *Atala* in the early 1880s, part of his often sappy romanticization of Christianity. And there is our own great Walt Whitman, whose *Song of Myself,* included in *Leaves of Grass* in 1855, celebrated the self so powerfully. And more recently, of course, in the bellowing tradition of the macho hunter, Ernest Hemingway shouting to a hunting partner in his

1935 *Green Hills of Africa*, "Bust the sonofabitch!," as the partner levels a high powered rifle at a slow-witted, myopic, leaf-eating creature, a rhinoceros. Hemingway's intention was to prove that manhood, and the esteem of others, is earned by slovenly, egoistic acts of killing. The animal in this case, of course, was not charging the hunter but trying to run away.

All of this sort of thing, the air of self-announcement and self-display, the turning of the world inside out, so that the ego becomes the axis upon which everything turns, is why T. E. Hulme, in his 1924 essays, *Speculations*, calls romanticism "spilt religion," a view that sees man as "intrinsically good, spoilt by circumstance; and the other [the classicist view] that he is intrinsically limited, but disciplined by order and tradition to something fairly decent. To the one party man's nature is like a well, to the other like a bucket."

Hulme goes on to refer to the "sane classical dogma of original sin," which the church adopted after the defeat of the Pelagian heresy. Pelagius had argued in the fifth century that St. Augustine was too pessimistic about human nature and that baptism was unnecessary because children were born innocent. No original sin, no need to wash it away. But that view of man merely shifts the focus of the argument to later life. The "evil leaven" is not neutralized.

During the great days of the philosophes, after the Christian God had been toppled, men like Wilde turned toward aesthetics to provide some sort of moral scaffolding in their lives. Some still do in the arts, though much of the arts has become so bizarre, cynical and tantrum ridden, that it is all too easily dismissed with a snicker or a yawn. It is a world that would have its rapture and its minimalist nullification of feeling at the same time. It is a place so confused and coarse, at times, that it cannot distinguish beauty from notoriety, or either one from money.

In the past, others such as Thomas Carlyle tried to use a theory of the Great Man to anchor things down, to quell the doubts. But the loss was felt and the disillusionment ran deep. It is said, for instance, that John Stuart Mill's efforts to construct utilitarianism, and to prove himself a stalwart reformer, living as he did from 1806 to 1873, doomed him to suffer from "pervasive emotions of loss, of absence, of [a feeling of] the unrecoverable."

Friedrich Nietzsche could only dismiss such disillusionment contemptuously by observing, "They are rid of the Christian God and now believe all the more firmly that they must cling to Christian morality." He proceeded to write such renowned works as *Thus Spake Zarathustra* in 1883 and *Beyond Good and Evil* in 1886, with a new man of the future in mind, someone who transcended the old values and emerged almost as another species. And he dreamed, as Unamuno says, of eternal recurrence, "that sorry counterfeit of immortality." As things turned out in the twentieth century tyrants proved to be the most eternally recurring thing of all.

No less a mind than that of Johann Wolfgang Goethe, who lived from 1749 to 1842, had cut directly to the bone on "doubt." "Doubt of any sort," he said, "cannot be removed except by action." Which may have something to do with his feeling uneasy, so Ortega claims at any rate, about his own "availability" in German courts, where some saw him as a learned amusement. Nonetheless, Goethe's comment is on target. Action can not only be used to remove doubt, it can be used as an excuse to transmute action into power.

Arbitrary use of political power, the exercise of Will, especially as the term "Will" came to be used by German romantics, from Johann Hamann and Johann Fichte to Adolf Hitler, can all too easily become a lethal, solitary exercise driven by a need for intensified sensation. It then becomes a kind of last ditch effort to verify existence itself, like psychopathic SS officers trying to fend off the fright of their own extinction by wading in pools of blood that prove they can be the cause of the extinction of others. And it involves the sort of engineering of instant tradition I referred to earlier, in this case something resembling the Aztec tradition of the skull-rack. Though in the case of the Aztec the skull-rack was woven into an ancient set of religious beliefs, theories of time, the place of the supernatural in daily life, and the roll of the seasons.

Which is not to justify the skull-rack approach to problem-solving, for the Aztec or the Nazi. But in the case of the Aztec there was ancestral help. For the Nazi that help came mostly from Dr. Goebbel's skills in the fabrication of toxic dramaturgy.

But the surrender to intensified personal sensation does little good without "ancestral help." It cannot be used, to fall back on Norbert Weiner's cybernetics language, as a means for "carrying out a certain operation [prediction] on the past." A Pater, a Wilde, a Henry Miller, all of the existentialist philosophers too, threaten always to maroon themselves in the dark spot, where the "evil leaven" resides, the place where Camus' *Stranger* found himself when he committed a meaningless murder.

But I would like to look, briefly again, at the role that romanticism plays in science. The romantic quality of science is often missed in historical interpretations of it, its romantic quality obscured by the excitement and rhetoric of progress. But this is not so in Irving Babbitt's *Rousseau and Romanticism*, published in 1919. He argues that romanticism began to divide in the eighteenth century into the emotional naturalism of romantic art and the utilitarian naturalism of science, technology and business. Both, he says, have roots in the presumption of human perfectibility.

Sometimes it all takes on a literal dreamy quality. Consider the plans some years ago to build an atomic breeder reactor at Clinch River. Millions of dollars and thousands of careers were involved. So were the dreams of the physicists. We hear Hans Bethe say of another prominent scientist involved in the plan, "Seaborg has said the breeder is an alchemist's dream. But maybe the fission-fusion hybrid is an even better dream."

Edward Teller said later that the "breeder was started by famous people who made the atomic bomb. And once you get [an idea like this] started, you cannot stop it. Vested interests become involved," including "scientists who put their whole lives into it. And they get indignant ["petulant" Ortega would say] if you propose an alternative."

It is this kind of romantic megalomania that put Oppenheimer at Almagordo, after the first bomb was exploded, quoting, in a grandiloquent way from the Upanishads, "Now I am become Death, the destroyer of worlds!", even as he "strode about like [the hero] from the movie *High Noon*." And thus the romantic image of scientist as hero takes form and is embraced by public sentiment. As Unamuno put it, "We would rather err with genius than hit the mark with the crowd."

The indignation that Teller refers to, or the postures of Oppenheimer at Almagordo, were also prominent in the great debate over "Star Wars" physics during the Reagan administration. In memoranda now made public many physicists acknowledged that Star Wars technology was considered by physicists to be far beyond the reach of technology at the time. Though the announcement of the program did cow the Soviets it held a dreamy kind of fascination for Reagan. But what is as notable is that Star War physicists have since said in television interviews that various Star Wars devices, the rail gun, the X-ray satellite idea that Teller touted before congressional committees, were "very exciting" in and of themselves. One physicist referred to his own experiences in the project as very like the delight children experience playing with toys.

Many readers, perhaps most, particularly scientists, because of the claim in science that science is a supposedly public or shared enterprise, would consider it preposterous to call science a romantic, existential enterprise. Yet, as we have seen, it is essentially an ego-driven, highly personal, rationalistic undertaking. It is intrinsically anti-traditional. Which means, if I am correct, that modern science and "ancestral help" are at odds. This means, as science's hold on the Western world view declines, or weakens, there will be a corresponding scurry toward the shadows of the non-rational, with all that implies, much of it repellent to the rationalist view of the world, even if it is saturated with meaning all its own.

Chapter 7

"Damnable and Detestable Curiosity"

I do not wish to claim that remarkable scientific and technological achievements have not taken place in the last several centuries. This is obvious in everything from medicine, moon-walking, computer science to smart bombs. Few of us fortunate enough to share in the benefits of these achievements, such as from those in medicine, would choose to give them up. Who among us is prepared, for instance, to surrender the blessings of medical anesthesia? But many of these great achievements are haunted by the "shadow of ourselves," by dangers as spectral and menacing as a volcano smoldering on the horizon.

Let me return to Pascal and Unamuno. Pascal says, in his *Pensees*, that "Curiosity is only vanity. Most frequently we wish to know but to talk." And this from Unamuno, from his 1921 *The Tragic Sense of Life*, "Curiosity, the so-called innate desire of knowing, only awakes and becomes operative after the necessity for the sake of living is satisfied . . . ."

Pascal gets to the heart of the issue in his usual rapier- like way. Unamuno, with his Spanish flourish uses more words, but also throws the entire question of knowing for knowing's sake, what we like to call "pure pursuit of truth," into stark relief, especially as these ideas are imbedded in the romantic view of life.

But take another illustration, from Denis Diderot of the early eighteenth century. He was the author of plays, pioneering works in art criticism and played a pivotal editorial role in the remarkable *Encyclopedie*. He was a wise man, and full of information. Yet he was able to write,

> One consideration especially that we ought never to lose from sight is that, if we ever banish man, or the thinking and contemplative being, from about the surface of the earth this pathetic spectacle of nature becomes no more than a scene of melancholy and silence ....

That the great spectacle of nature is somehow "pathetic" unless it is contemplated by homo sapiens sounds strange indeed.

Or consider Claude Saint-Simon again. In the eighteenth and early nineteenth century, even though little was really understood of the lives of people outside the immediate Western culture, he concluded that we could "affirm in advance" what a good society should become, and that "We do not even hesitate to say that the Europeans alone are able to teach the Indians their history." It did not occur to such men as Saint-Simon that an Indian tribe's history is encoded in its customs and traditions.

I want to approach the question of curiosity from a cybernetic standpoint, as if curiosity was a scanning function such as a radar dish performs. We might say then that a radar dish is "curious" about the position of its target. Carrying the analogy a step further we might say that curiosity is similar to, if not identical with, consciousness itself. We might even go further and say that it is the "irritation of doubt," a "privation of habit," that generates consciousness in us. And we respond to finding our target, finding out what we know, as the radar system might. We lock on and give the system over to routine, that is, form habits. Egoistic needs may, of course, upset socially shaped habits, which was the reason presumably that Denis Diderot saw everything going silent and melancholy unless humans were busily perceiving it. Which is rather like the ideas of some Christian philosophers who claimed that the universe was maintained by God's consciousness.

We are a curious species, but far less curious as a species than we in the West think is the case with all members of our species. We cite the "conquest" of Mount Everest, for instance, to try to make the point, with the strange species-centric conviction that the poor, old mountain cares one way or the other. Or we cite the impressive voyages of Captain James Cook, meddling about in the Pacific. The fact is, however, most humans are not driven by some, deep, profound need to know what is out there beyond the next valley or mountain. Colin Turnbull, for instance, tells us of some Mbuti pygmy who felt intense anxiety and the strong desire to go back home when they walked out of their forest home into an unfamilar landscape.

Most humans, and most other creatures for that matter, are curious in the sense of Romer's Rule. Left to themselves, they try to keep out of trouble. They do not stick their noses into hornets' nests to find out what makes hornets tick, but to locate honey. And contrary to what space scientists would have us believe, there is little inside our species that makes it imperative to know whether Pluto is made of gas, volcanic stone, brick or tallow.

But lest I be accused of writing like some cranky Luddite, let me say that I too thrill looking at photographs taken by space vehicles, and of the pictures of the tiny worlds inhabited by microbes. I thrill too when I watch a good television broadcast of a documentary prepared by field biologists, obviously at great cost in money and infinite patience. But I know many people that yawn at the photograph of some newly discovered distant star. I know some who are totally unmoved by the recent finding of a Mars meteorite with signs of microbe-like life in it.

I wish to suggest that we should try to see Western man not just as a creature given to outbursts of curiosity, for all sorts of historical and cultural reasons, but that we should also see him as a creature convinced of his perfectibility and frequently feverishly nosing about so that his ego is reassured. In most cultures unbounded curiosity is hedged about by all sorts of taboos and Thou Shalt Nots! which often act as sociological stabilizers, bizarre and cruel though they may sometimes be.

Further, when we remind ourselves, as the sciences remind us continuously, that the universe is infinitely complex and that each discovery "poses more questions than it answers," we are obviously caught in an infinite regress in which satisfying curiosity is dendritic, fanning out in all directions, ad infinitum. But as it fans out, ad infinitum, it becomes increasingly difficult to hold "information" together in a culturally coherent, meaningful configuration, and then pay for more of it. As the ideomass expands into ever thinner slices of specialist-driven ideas, the problems of values, the priorities that inevitably make knowing one thing more important than knowing another, intensify. That is why I believe it is possible, in principle at least, to predicate the existence of cultural cognitive carrying capacity.*

---

*The idea of cultural cognitive carrying capacity is a complicated idea better left for development elsewhere. What I believe it comes down to is that the number of cognitive propositions that can be held together meaningfully, in a given ideomass, that is to say, stitched together by values that give them meaning, is governed by laws similar to those that determine carrying capacity of information inherent to living systems generally. This is implied in ecological information theory as employed by such ecologists as Ramon Margalef. This could account for the rise, flourishing and decline of many cultural phenomena, such as art forms, literature movements and scientific information itself, all discussed in one way or the other by A. L. Kroeber, Oswald Spengler, Brooks Adams, F. Stuart Chapin and others who see, in Chapin's terms, "societal reaction patterns" that follow sygmoidal growth patterns similar to other natural growth forms. I see support for this idea in the work of cognitive anthropologists such as A. Kimball Romney who has measured "efficient" or "short path" associations in free-listed words, such as animal names used in English and Spanish. When information associations are stretched beyond the capacity of a culture's value system to hold them together meaningfully, which is to say, when their efficient or "short path" relationship becomes too costly, the ideomass begins to come apart at the value "seams." At any rate, I think some such application of information and systems theory helps us understand why cultures "rise and fall," relative to their information bank and energy exploitation practices seen broadly.

The reader may wish to examine my thoughts along these lines in a paper I

Values, the axiological glue that makes some information useful and other information irrelevant or useless, we call "meaning." Meaning is what binds modes of institutional life, economic, religious, political and the like, together. If an economic activity, for instance, takes on a meaning all its own, as might be the case in all-out, ruthless quest for money, terms like greed and avarice will come into play as evidence of countervailing taboos, announcing themselves often in religious or political form. This is one of the reasons that Christianity and capitalism are often such uneasy bedfellows, a point made by Max Weber in 1920 in his *Protestant Ethic and the Spirit of Capitalism.* Calvinism, in particular, the argument goes, deflected ostentatious consumption of wealth into reinvestment, triggering a positive feedback economic process.

In any case, extreme specialization such as we see going on all around us carries its own costs, its built-in hazards. Note how this works. Ortega aptly labeled the new creature of extreme specialization a "learned ignoramus," someone who knows everything about very little. But such "ignoramity," if I may coin a rather ugly term, is not proportionately subjugated by humility, wisdom or respect for what goes on in "the shadows." The learned ignoramus, says Ortega, displays a kind of "petulance." That was what Edward Teller meant when he said atomic physicists dislike being told what they cannot afford.

The petulance of the science community was the subject of a recent comment in *Science*, in July, 1995. It had to do with debates over reductions in federal support for the sciences and

---

published in *Human Ecology*, edited by Frederick Sergent II published in Amsterdam in 1974. I suggest in that paper, called "Human Behavior: Some Biological and Cultural Determinants," that because evolution, cosmic as well as biological, operates by a kind of *fait accompli* strategy, it can really run in but one direction, toward every greater complexity. Reversed, it disappears. That is why long-run rather than short-run survival becomes the ultimate test of living systems. I appreciate the circular nature of this argument. "That we are, not what we are" remains the great philosophical question behind the entire matter. Elements of this position are also found in my book, *The Death of Progress* (see the bibliography in this volume).

was called, interestingly enough, "Is Science Lobbying an Oxymoron?" Physicist Alan Bromley, former science adviser to President Bush, is quoted as saying, "A combination of arrogance and ignorance" stands in the way of effective lobbying by the nation's physicists. "The arrogance," says Bromley, "comes from a feeling that politicians should not question the value of science's contribution to society." The report then quotes Daniel Goldin, head of NASA: "Why is it so hard for the science and technology community to understand their customer is the American public?"

The reason, of course, is that science is what *Science* magazine has dubbed it, a "Culture of Credit," where a "tremendous premium is placed on individual credit." It is a place where "Credit is a bottomless pit--there's never enough for most people."

Were scientists asked to work anonymously, like artisans carving gargoyles for a medieval cathedral, most of the scientific enterprise would freeze where it stands. That is why plagiarism becomes such an issue in today's academic community, as in the recent case reported in *Science*, May 1995, in which the plaintiff scientist won a false claims case and was awarded $550,000. Her university was required to pay. Another issue of *Science*, in May of 1995, devoted an entire section to the problems of assuring that scientists "get credit" for their research.

And all this in spite of the fact that in the sciences discoveries can come so fast that an individual's ideas can be forgotten in the wink of an eye. Which can account in part too for the almost nihilistic attitudes toward anything "old" in lives driven by an egoistic quest for fame. In the face of impending irrelevance, a kind of cruel death all its own, the individual has little choice but to remain forever optimistic about his or her "contribution."

There is undoubtedly an inherent sense of reward in discovering something significantly new, in the sciences or not. One need, however, only recall the expeditions of Scott, Amundsen or Byrd to the Poles, and the privations they underwent in the process, to appreciate how potent an element the ego is in "discovery," even if, as in the case of the Poles, the

Poles were discovered long before shivering humans showed up. The North Pole was not unknown to the polar bear and the South Pole was not news to the penguin. The odd thing is that human discovery" is presumed to somehow raise the ontological status of whatever it is that is "discovered."

The quest for fame is probably as old as the human race, at least recently evolved versions of it. But in the culture of science it is an extremely prominent force, the sort of thing that put Oppenheimer, metaphorically at any rate, in *High Noon*. So it is not difficult to see why the old Christian image of man, slogging his way through a vale of tears, tormented most of the time, praying only for a happy death and eternal life among a choir of harp-strumming angels, so put off the philosophes and burgeoning science. The pessimism that "original sin" represents is the very opposite of the romantic optimism required for the everlasting "pursuit of scientific truth."

Consider the ill-fated Supercollider-Superconductor particle physics project that was being built in Texas, at a cost of some eleven billion dollars. It was intended to help curious scientists get to the bottom of the cosmic order, all those enigmatic particles and forces that make the universe such an inspiring mystery to mankind. There was even talk among some physicists who admired the remarkable work of cosmologist Stephen Hawkings, author of *A Short History of Time*, that SCSC would finally allow us to figure out what God was up to when He triggered the Big Bang. But the money for SCSC ran out. The project collapsed in a heap of second-guesses about its costs, which is to say its value. The project did not determine what held the cosmos together. It had to settle for the discovery, not really all that impressive as a discovery, that large amounts of public money hold the universe of professional physicists together.

Or consider the SETI project, the Search for Extraterrestrial Intelligence. With intelligent life on earth in obvious short supply, its champions proposed that we find it on heavenly bodies thousands of light years from our planet by using expensive radio telescopes. We would listen for signals from outer space and we would beam them into outer space, then wait a few thousand years for a response. But the project went under, at least the federally supported segment of it, because money was needed for less glamorous things, like new and bigger prisons, more police on the neighborhood beat and removal of graffiti from gang-infested sections of our great cities.

The egoistic nature of so many scientific enterprises explains their megalomaniac quality. An international team of physicists, Alvaro De Rujula, George Charpak, Sheldon Glashow and Robert Wilson proposed in 1983, according to *Science*, "one of the most ambitious [projects] ever conceived by our species." The GEOTRON would "scan the solid earth with neutrinos much as a physician scans the human body with x-rays ... a kind of whole earth tomography, analogous to the computerized tomography used in medicine." The costs would run well into the billions. The idea was to look for gas, oil and minerals. The proposed project "rivals the construction of the pyramids." Which is all well and good, and could still happen. The question would remain, however, What about all those wretched people wandering the earth's surface living the sort of lives that Kaplan describes in *To the Ends of the Earth*? Let them eat neutrinos?

Or take proposals, mercifully few, of those who suggest that we get rid of thousands of useless atomic warheads by firing them into the sun. A bold and expensive plan with one fatal flaw, the tendency for space vehicles occasionally to blow up at launch. So we now find that dismantling and storing atomic warheads more costly and difficult than inventing and manufacturing them in the first place. We needed perhaps five hundred warheads to assure the incineration of any potential enemy. To be on the safe side we built twenty thousand. Soviet experts reasoned in an equally cogent fashion. Now everyone is concerned that a lunatic or fanatic will acquire one by hook or crook and hold an entire nation hostage. By putting a small warhead into a small trunk, renting a small fishing boat for a few dollars, the fanatic could row up the East River of Manhattan, or the Thames, and hymning to his favorite God, blow a city to dust.

There is something else involved. It has to do with the idea that Emerson, and others, expressed when he said, "We kill in order to dissect." This is not merely a comment on the killing of animals in order to do research on them. A case can be made for the humane dispatch of animals, for instance, in a veterinary school, so that doctors might better reduce the misery of far more animals as a result. For example, a vaccine for rinderpest, which kills cattle slowly and painfully, was the result of animal research. A vaccine for deadly feline leukemia was similarly developed by research on cats.

Still, it is not easy to miss the terrible irony of so much of our concern for animal well-being. Scientists complain that the rate of animal extinction now being brought about by tropical deforestation is accelerating at such a pace that by the time global population hits about 11 billion, some say around 2135, at least five, perhaps as high as 30 million species will become extinct. This will be "the largest of the mass extinctions of the geological record," says *Science* in a 1986 "News and Comment" piece, meanwhile, deploring the fact that "in most cases [this will occur] before individual species become known to science." It is as if humankind's knowing that it exists is the reason for a species' existence. In this case, I suppose, we might dub this reasoning "the Diderot effect."

However, I refer to something more subtle and more sinister. It is the swaggering assumption, going back to early Christianity in the West, and assuming its more species-centric form in the thinking of persons such as Thomas Aquinas and Rene Descartes, that humans are higher on the ladder of being than other forms of life and that the animals really do not feel pain in the sense that humans do. There follows the conclusion that rational man makes progress, and gets to heaven, while other species must wait patiently for slow and jerky evolution to raise them up from the slime.

Those assumptions are all too often used as license to use animals in ways far more troubling than just slaughtering and eating them. After all, the food chain is not a human invention, and if Anybody is to get credit for that macabre invention it is not mankind. Even the plants, as David Attenborough illustrates so well in his recent *The Private Life of Plants*, are party to the food chains' odd, remorseless rule over living things.

But it is when our curiosity about nature becomes a licentious act of self-indulgence that real mischief is underway. The self-indulgent dimension of investigation, regardless of the pain that it inflicts on other life forms, can then hide behind the wish not just to know, but to talk, as Pascal would say, to preen our egos. This preening, this sin against consciousness, presents the moral problem of curiosity-without-taboos in high relief.

Should we find out if distant stars have planetary systems or should we spend the money trying to prevent extinction of the gorilla? Since we cannot afford everything, all such questions become questions of priorities, values. As the degradation of the world's ecological order becomes more obvious, so do these questions of priorities, of values.

Such questions of priority were ignored for a long time in the "progress" culture simply because it was busy looting the planet of riches thought to be inexhaustible. But it is notable that even during the nineteenth century considerable "irritation of doubt" about the exercise of unfettered curiosity already existed among great scientists.

Let me cite a letter from no less than Charles Darwin on the issue of vivisection. In it he writes a colleague concerning the work of a French scientist.

> You ask about my opinion on vivisection. I quite agree that it is justifiable for real investigations on physiology; but not for mere damnable and detestable curiosity. It is a subject that makes me sick with horror, and I will not say another word about it, else I shall not sleep tonight.

The important thing to notice here is that Darwin tries valiantly to make a distinction between "real investigation" and "mere damnable and detestable curiosity."

That is no easy distinction to make, and Darwin fails in the trying. It is only when we use gross illustrations that the distinction becomes somewhat clearer. Consider researchers who sew the eyelids of kittens shut so that the researchers might record how the creatures respond to light in adulthood. "Research on blindness and its causes!" some announce. But whose blindness? Or consider the wildlife researcher at a Big Ten university who broke the wings of waterfowl to see if they could survive as cripples in the wild. Of course, the kittens or geese are not now called simply kittens or geese. In science, they are "animal models." And inflicting pain or punishment, of course, is called "negative reinforcement."

It should be noted in the latter case of geese "models," much publicized in 1982, that the senior researcher supervising the project argued to the press that the mistake was not in mangling the animals but in allowing the research report to reach the press and the public. Which is to say that a highly personal, solipsistic, definition of morality was used to justify an act of obvious cruelty, arrantly stupid though it was as "research."

A passage from Paul Feyerabend's 1975 book *Against Method*, a volume that caused quite a stir at the time, illustrates the extreme degree to which scientific curiosity, what Unamuno called the "rabid mania for originality," begins to justify itself as a matter of ego and little else.

Feyerabend quotes from the British journal *Lancet* in which a renowned biologist, Dr. Szentgyorgi, says,

> The desire to alleviate suffering is of small value in research. Such a person should be advised to work for charity. Research wants egoists, damned egoists, who seek their own pleasure and satisfaction, but find it in solving the problems of nature.

My intention in noting this Dr. Frankenstein-like thought is not simply to point a finger, since it is not really clear whether the comment was made seriously or in jest. It seems to have been made with a straight face. Nature, we may add, has been "solving her problems" for eons, without the help of such as Dr. Szentgyorgi.

In a gentler, more innocent vein, I might note the remark of the Nobel Prize winning physicist Subrahmayan Chandrasekhar. He says, "I never ask if any area is important [for research], only if I can construct a body of knowledge that pleases me."

The problem, once again, is that real investigation of the sort Darwin had tried to justify, and damnable and detestable curiosity, cannot be easily separated. Both usually predicate a special license for "damned egoists" merely to amuse themselves. Which makes it hard to justify real investigation without falling back upon some sort of social definition, to distinguish what is real from what is detestable, Frankenstein's hyperrationalism, an almost pornographic scientific curiosity, from a less subjective definition of it. Which can lead to all sorts of curiously overblown claims for what the "scientific outlook" can do for man.

And it produces in scientists as renowned and respected as E. O. Wilson, the entomologist, the following sort of assertion. I take it from his book, *On Human Nature*, published in 1978.

Pure knowledge is the ultimate emancipator. It equalizes people and sovereign states, erodes the archaic barriers of superstition and promises to lift the trajectory of cultural evolution.

There is unfortunately little evidence that this is true. The opposite would seem closer to the truth. The French Enlightenment, for instance, was drowned in a sea of blood during the Terror. "Pure knowledge" in weapons physics, on the other hand, has merely raised the trajectory of intercontinental missiles. Our fear of nuclear proliferation and terrorism is another fruit of pure knowledge. And pure knowledge has yet to tell us what to do with the tide of lethal radioactive waste now building up around the world, not to mention problems of global warming, the extinction of species and the life of increasing numbers of humans living in the shanty-town "misery belts" strangling large cities like Mexico City or Cairo. The "archaic barriers of superstition" that Wilson refers to were often blind, functionless beliefs. But that was frequently not the case. In many cases they were, in fact, negative feedback processes at work in the shadows of cultural non-consciousness.

The fact is that a romantic interpretation of science and technology has pitched us into the dark spot, no less obviously than it did at the time of Condorcet or Carlyle. Such purity has no moral frame around it, no ethical field upon which it can be placed to judge its social meaning, indeed, more fundamentally, its ecological meaning. Ultimately it becomes a thin slice of personal experience, that of a hermit's definition of a world that has shrunken to a fugitive, self-centered thing, empty of significance except for its terrible potential for misuse.

I might note here too that Irving Babbitt, author of *Rousseau and Romanticism*, a man who died before the horrors of the Nazi concentration camps, reminded us that romantic subjectivization of experience can drive us toward "efficient megalomania," the sort of thing we witnessed in the Third Reich. He warned also that the romantic lust for power can end, in Edmund Burke's phrase, with an urge to "improve the mystery of murder." In the Nazi camps there were also, after all, research problems to be solved.

In any case, I believe we can see meta-rational processes at work in human affairs all around us. Some are grim and remorseless. Others are more benign on the surface, such as the collapse of animal husbandry among people of the Sahel, where desertification is moving steadily southward in West Africa. In other cases we aid and abet what the rest of nature is doing, as with conservation movements, colluding with Nature. The "deep ecology" movement, for example, which begins in America with men like John Muir and Aldo Leopold, amounts to a new form of animism. Animism is not rational. But it has a meta-rational function. It reaches beyond human concerns into the web of life, into that mysterious logic that holds Nature itself together.

This is why there has been a spate of new books having to do with the ethics of human use of animals, hunting, trapping, riding, branding, dissecting, taming, capturing, torturing and killing them. Gary L. Francione's recent *Animals, Property and*

the Law is an example. So is Andrew Linzey's *Animal Theology*
Francione is a law professor at Rutgers University and Linzey is
a well known theologian. To my knowledge, neither is an
extremist. But both are concerned with the limits on humans in
their use of animals. They represent the rise of an entire new
range of taboos in human relations with the rest of the biological
world.

Consider the recent observation by Hugh Honour in an essay
on Burma in the July 1995 issue of the *New York Review of
Books*. He notes that Burmese farmers welcomed new fertilizers
and rice paddy cultivation techniques because they allowed them
to cut the number of paddy fields by half and thus allowed more
time for meditation. Which response, he notes, astonished
economists who rank Burma as one of the ten poorest countries
in the world. But meditation has in this case, a negative
feedback effect on pell-mell "development" of Burmese rice
paddies. It sanctifies a meta-rational response to "poverty." In
a strange way it protects the functions of this poverty from the
economists to whom meditation has no meaning.

In the sciences, resanctification is having profound braking,
i.e., negative feedback, effects. A recent issue of *Science*, one of
the June 1995 issues, carried a news report called "Who Owns
the Past?" It summarized new, severe restrictions, new taboos,
on archeological study of ancient human bones. They have been
imposed by native Tasmanian groups, by Orthodox Jews of
Israel, by Australian aborigines and by Native American
organizations. A spokesman for one of these groups asks, "What
ever gave scientists the notion that their values are more
important than ours?" So entire museum collections of bones
have been removed from museums for reburial by these native
organizations. And, it should be noted, these reburial demands
have been supported in the courts.

And in a kind of farcical amplification of the issue of
patenting genetically altered strains of mice, so called
"knockouts," a recent issue of *Science*, in November of 1995, is
titled "Scientists Attacked for 'Patenting' Pacific Tribe." It was
an article devoted to the work of a group of scientists working

with the Hagahai tribe of Papua, New Guinea, under auspices of the National Institutes of Health. The researchers were accused by critics of "stealing Hagahai genes." "Is Nothing Sacred?" demanded one newspaper.

Researchers had patented a virus-infected cell line of Hagahai blood, in the hope of preventing the spread of a lethal disease known as pigbel, related perhaps to malaria, malnutrition, AIDS and ecological degradation. Researchers had applied for a patent on a human T cell leukemia virus of the Hagahai variant, insisting that they had discussed the patent with the Hagahai and had arrived at a "clear understanding" of "ownership." Insisted one spokesman, "I think that rights of people in the Third World should be respected when biological discoveries of potential commercial benefit are made from biological samples of any kind." The key term here, of course, is "commercial." The patent was approved on March 14, 1995.

But news of the event leaked via Internet, of course, and critics appeared on every side. Said one, "Once you allow patenting of any life form, you pretty much end up patenting all life forms." And so, as in the case of Robert Oppenheimer, scientists had once again collided, almost accidentally, with the idea of limits to rationality.

Taboos sometimes begin to appear in curious ways. A recent, 1996, editorial in *Science* magazine, the official organ of the American Association for the Advancement of Science, something I may not have noted earlier in citing it as a source, begins by saying, "The era of generous and stable federal funding of science, long taken for granted, is over." In essence, this says that science can no longer forage amidst what seemed to many of them as a social and economic environment of virtually unlimited resources. The editorial then counsels scientists to give up their precious ways, and their political naivete, to become political activists. Which means the end of the idea of science as simply the exercise of subsidized "idle curiosity," which is what Thorstein Veblen said universities were for in 1918, when he wrote his caustic *The Higher Learning in America: A Memorandum on the Conduct of Universities by*

Business Men. Veblen saw big money as an enemy of free inquiry.

His arguments may seem both naive and unnecessarily vitriolic now. But he was dealing with conflicting sanctified values. Now, as money seems to be running low, or at least harder to come by, the conflict between subsidized "idle curiosity" and foraging for money is probably clearer in some ways. But what is going on is perhaps more subtle. We see deeper meta-rational functions at work, for instance, in Jeremy Rifkin's Foundation for Economic Trends and his zealous efforts to stop scientists from patenting life forms. What Rifkin is doing, from the standpoint of my argument here, is to "upgrade" (I use the word "upgrade" deliberately) laws to the status of taboos strong enough to make the actual patent laws he is fighting irrelevant.

There are other obvious cases of this sort of non-rational factor at work. They include resanctification of broad expanses of institutional life, such as the spontaneous reassemblage of sex-role taboos in non-western cultures lurching toward religious fundamentalism. The re-establishment of taboos is, after all, what the present debate in America over control of sexual vulgarity and violence on television is all about.

Max Oelschlaeger comes close to making this point about taboos in the book I cited, *The Idea of Wilderness*. But he does not carry his argument all the way. Taboos often have ecological functions. That is commonly observed in anthropology. The taboos that work survive, but only if they work over the long haul. But taboos are by their very nature non-rational. They operate in the "shadows."

This is what men like Aldo Leopold and John Muir talk of when they refer to our "obligations" to use land wisely. When these obligations harden into a commandment or a taboo, they rule as habits. When absorbed into habit, into tradition, into "the way it has always been done," into the meta-rational, they not only chafe less, but they lower the costs of constant conscious attention.

We may note how a supposedly simple matter of the "truth" becomes entangled in issues of ethics, egos and commercial advantage, none of which are supposed to be involved in pure science. For despite the claims that science is a social process and that progress in it is only possible when information is shared, it also mythologizes objectivity and magnifies the importance of recognition. All of which is very evident to those outside science, lawmakers in particular, when questions of budgets, that is priorities, come up. The myth of the pursuit of "pure knowledge" can then collapse in a sardonic tableau.

"Meaning," an idea or habit to which value is affixed, is, after all, what the pragmatists meant when they argued that the use of an idea determines its meaning. I might quote Peirce again. "To develop [an idea's] meaning, we have, therefore, simply to determine what habits it produces, for what a thing means is simply what habits it involves."

This is what is involved with the rise of new taboos in science. Since we can no longer afford to do everything that scientists want to do a good deal of hand-wringing takes place. What this hand-wringing represents is the irritation of doubt and the end of an illusion. And in an ironic way it perhaps represents the expanding rule of meta-rationality.

Chapter 8

A Daunting Paradox

I think it is possible to peer into the future, shrouded in mist and conjecture though it may be, by reading some of the more insightful anthropologists. They show us how tribal systems can serve as miniature laboratories in which we see how Nature takes the measure of human habits.

Reading Roy Rappaport's *Pigs for the Ancestors*, a 1968 book about his research among the Tsembaga tribe of New Guinea (he lived among these people in 1962 and 1963), I was struck by several thoughts in particular. One is the thought that mankind has not lived as part of a climax ecological order for something like ten thousand years, since the Neolithic, the New Stone Age.

A climax ecological order is a mature system, usually relatively stable, slowly changing and often complex, an old growth forest, for instance, or a long-established desert or a stable tide water area. And the evidence is, indeed, that humans have been pushing the earth's total ecosystem toward simplification and instability for a very long time.

At first these changes would have been slow and slight. Max Oelschlager believes that the great divide between man and nature actually began to form with the domestication of grain.

It allowed people to stay in one place longer, to store surpluses and to build cities, many fortified to protect what had been stored. And since that time human modification of the ecosystem has speeded up, in the last thousand years in particular. The speed of change is now so fast that it has precipitated the kinds of problems that Malthus saw on the near horizon just a few hundred years ago.

The purpose of this human intervention has been to speed natural processes, seeding, tilling, harvesting and such. Which means that thermodynamically the entire process began to heat up. It also means that primitive peoples are swept aside, often simply obliterated, when they come in contact with high-speed cultures, "developed" cultures. And seemingly simple, seemingly beneficial, changes such as replacement of stone axes with metal axes can have profound effects on the simpler, vulnerable cultures.

Lauriston Sharp, in 1952, showed just how overwhelming this sort of change can be. He describes how the introduction of metal axes by missionaries to the Yir Yorant people of Australia sent shock waves through the entire native culture. The metal axe not only upset day-to-day hacking, cutting and chopping practices, it tore into complex religious behavior surrounding the symbolic manufacture and significance of stone axes. The authority structure of the tribe was affected, indeed its entire political system.

This is not a new sort of story, to be sure. Missionaries, rifles and whisky, often in combination, tore apart the fabric of many North American Indian tribes and left them pauperized and hopeless. In many cases devastating epidemics moved along with the missionaries, trappers and settlers, and at other times outpaced them.

There is probably no better concise description of this whole wretched business than John Bodley's 1982 *Victims of Progress*. The slave trade, exploitation of coffee, tea and mining labor, not to mention indiscriminant slaughter of bison, elephants and other species, were part of this unfolding series of crimes against tribal people living as they had, more or less, since the Old Stone Age.

The point is that from a long-term standpoint primitive cultures were often far more stable ecologically than modern culture. Like an old growth forest, or stable tidal zone, they went on for centuries with little rapid change, certainly little by comparison with modern culture. And from this standpoint the ideal ecosystem for humankind is something like an Old Stone Age climax order, thermodynamically cooler and able to last a very long time. Most of us prefer, needless to say, to keep the thought of our living such lives in comic strips.

The anthropologist Robin Fox has referred, wittily, to the Old Stone Age, the paleolithic, as the "paleoterrific." And one of the things that makes that prehistoric time so "terrific," he suggests, is that it could "go on forever," that it ran "cool." By comparison our present system with its enormous extra energy input, petroleum especially, runs "hot."

One need but fly across America at night and view the millions of lights in our cities and towns to appreciate what a thermodynamically "hot" culture looks like from thirty thousand feet away. In fact, our use of petroleum, coal and natural gas has amounted to puncturing the skin of the planet, draining fuel to the surface, and setting the flooded surface on fire. And one of the cruel ironies of "development" is that regardless of what is done to stop pollution and energy waste, if there is not a radical reduction in population, and therefore, presumably energy use per capita, the problem of ventilating the earth's heat into space remains.

It may be possible, of course, for a highly technological ecological order similar to modern culture to go on forever, provided its population is low enough for it to take its place within other mature, natural systems. Which leads one to suspect that the very existence of cities is evidence that they presently run too hot to survive in the long run. Cities may actually be pathological symptoms of an over-saturated human population level. As such they may be seen as enormous energy sinks into which excess numbers of our species go to die.

This puts a pretty grim face on cities, I would be the first to admit, especially on their legendary appeal to yokels from the country. That hot city life has a strong appeal to young country folk is legendary. And there are now the powerful economic forces that attract people into the cities and off of the land. Kaplan talks a good deal about these forces in his *To the Ends of the Earth.*

The fact that cities run hot from a strict energy consumption point of view helps explain why many collapse, disintegrate and often dramatically disappear. Sometimes they simply exhaust the resources in their immediate environs, then spend so much energy in long distance foraging and trade that they "meet themselves coming back" as the saying goes.

The story of the collapse of the twelfth century Indian city of Cahokia, Illinois (it numbered about 15,000) comes to mind because recent archeological reports indicate that it decimated its hinterland forests for fortification timber, only to be overwhelmed by flooding and crop failure. Something similar seems to have been involved in the collapse of many ancient cities such as the Mayan temple centers of Palenque and Tikal, and perhaps the great temple cities of Cambodia and Thailand. There is a lot of debate about particulars, but it appears increasingly probable that ecological factors were the basic forces that put an end to their hot life.

Fox notes that literacy itself is a measure of a hot culture. He reminds us that literacy is a late intrusion in human life on the planet and that it is probably overvalued inasmuch as humans got along well for many thousands of years without it.

Another measure of a hot culture is its level of self-consciousness. Literacy, and now high-speed electronic communication, heats up such self-consciousness. Which means that the "irritation of doubt" heats up our lives. On the other hand, traditions, customs, habits help cool things down. Cities, of course, are not conducive to living by habit.

Technically, however, an ecologically hot system and a cognitively hot system are up against the same thermodynamic laws. I need not get into that complicated question here except to say that cognition is not exempt from the laws of entropy any more than a field of wheat or a forest.

It is Fox's argument, further, that the great teachers such as Buddha, Christ, Mohammed, Thomas More and Gandhi, all urged a return to "paleo-morality," a return to the "communal ethic of the tribelet," that is, to social systems that think cool. This is not to be taken as an idealization of a noble savage. "But we are talking," he says, "of what is accepted as a moral ideal, either explicitly in codes or implicitly in custom and myth." Which is to say that codes, customs and myths are encoded information, memory without consciousness, memory as a predictor.

But there is another side to this matter of codes, customs and myths, what I have called memory without consciousness. It is that many deep ecological functions are often protected from individual rationality by sanctified, collective, non-rational behaviors. In the Tsembaga case, their ritual cycle of pig slaughter, pork distribution, cessation of intertribal warfare, ritualized courtship dancing, practices that are called the "kaiko" cycle, are suffused with taboos and sanctified beliefs that prevent the individual from really "understanding," in a rationalist sense, what the whole thing is about. The "kaiko" is an ecological regulator that runs in cycles, depending on how fast pig herds expand and trigger ritual slaughter.

What is important to note about the "kaiko" is that sanctification of many of its components puts them outside the reach of individual rational examination, so that individuals do not appreciate the costs of their best, long-term interests. *The group's long-run interests are masked by sanctification, and this sanctification deflects rational, immediate, personal pursuit of gain.* A degree of ignorance of the long-term "meaning" of it all allows deeper meta-rational functions to survive. Contrary to what we in the West now so commonly assume, the sum of individual, immediate self-interests may not be the same as the best, long-term interest of all.

But surely this has profound implications for the relationships of non-reason and reason in our lives. If a degree of ignorance of the "meaning" of the great swirl and twist of events around us is required for our survival, what does this say of the very idea of "reason?" Therein lies the great paradox. We are not omniscient, and it is improbable that we will ever be, despite the pomps of science. Omniscience is reserved for the gods, or some of them. So is "masking" a form of "wisdom?" If it is, we are caught within a philosophic snarl that one would not wish even upon a full-time philosopher, friend or not.

But the "masking" process is reminiscent of Hardin's argument in *The Tragedy of the Commons*. In that paper he shows why individual concern for short-term advantage blocks individual understanding of the larger social good. In his illustrations, Hardin notes that although the individual can see clearly enough the advantage of stuffing one more sheep into a commons, he does not see the long-run damage to the commons when every one is equally "rational."

Which will bring to mind, of course, the difficulty we have in the United States convincing ranchers that overloading federal land, the western grazing commons, is unwise. Many ranchers insist it is a matter of individual freedom from socialist meddling. This means that the idea of "freedom" has become sanctified and that it prevents the rancher from recognizing where his own best long-range interests lie. Without values that sanctify some notion of the common good, such as patriotism might, or respect for "God's creation," it is virtually impossible to control individual "rational" selfishness. And the reason is very like Pascal insisting that reason is "averse" to recognizing its own limits.

The masking function of sanctified beliefs is to prevent deeper, long-range ecological regulators, what I refer to as meta-rational processes, from falling victim to the dissolvent powers of individual reason. When we take an "enlightened" view of self-interest it means, in other words, that self-interest, selfishness, has been transformed by a masking process, into its "enlightened" status.

I would like to insert another illustration from anthropology. O. K. Moore has suggested that scapulimancy (the reading of burnt caribou shoulder blades in divination practices) among the Neskapi Indians of Canada performs the same kind of masking function, though he does not call it masking. But he says the practice randomizes hunting patterns and slows, or prevents, overkill of caribou. It works, in other words, because it is *not* a good predictor. Some argue that this is true of a great many soothsaying practices and hosts of "superstitions." They persist because of occasional reinforcement, not because they "make sense" as good predictors. Many of them only "make sense" at a meta-rational level.

Interestingly enough, something like this problem of reason trying to outsmart itself for its own good is implicit to the venerable old economic *laissez faire* principle of the "hidden hand" at work in a "free" market. Of course, if the hand were really hidden, it could not be understood. Or if someone were to unmask the hidden hand, as decision theorists like to think they can, the whole principle collapses in upon itself.

The assumption of an actual "free" market is that thousands of small "rational" market decisions are a safer bet than a few big decisions that, so to speak, bet the farm. This implies that foolishness in day-to-day decisions is best diluted by spreading it over time and that centralized foolishness is dangerous. Which accords, indeed, with good ecological theory. For the "hidden hand" argument is a meta-rational argument. It is also tinctured with a deep suspicion of human reason itself. It is, if you will, an illustration of the kind of "masking" process I have been talking about. Unfortunately, that does not excuse it from Malthusian forces, since breeding habits are themselves day-to-day decisions, or night-by-night, and there is seldom much that is rational about it.

Consider a fictional case that illustrates my point. A fisherman with a fine, new electronic fishfinder suddenly realizes that the "efficiency" of his fishfinder is responsible for the decline of his catch. He destroys his own device and also those of others in his fleet. He suspects that if he does not destroy the equipment of his friends, one of them may well go about secretly using his own fishfinder, and devil take the hindmost. Is he a paranoid Luddite or a meta-rationally wise man? Without some sort of sanctified collective notion of "the greater good" he becomes a paranoid loner.

Reason must allow itself to be outwitted because it does not trust itself? A daunting paradox if ever there was one. For how do we analyze, or at least understand, what takes place in the shadows, that vast and mysterious penumbra surrounding reason, a place of wizards, angels, demons, comedians, thieves, lovers, conjurers, murderers, priests, messiahs, and savants, a place saturated with sanctifications and often screened by the ineffable? All we can do, I suppose, is sketch the outlines of what we seem to see brooding in the half-lit future.

Chapter 9

The Twenty-First Century
as a Fourth World

There are probably more population experts on earth than any other type of expert, with the exceptions perhaps of sex experts and auto repairmen. But if they are correct (the population experts, I mean), humankind is rather like a weed species. By the middle of the twenty-first century it will have over-run just about ever square inch of the planet and things cannot but take a turn for the worse. Of course, this may not happen. Only a fool tries to be precise about the future.

In any case, the earth can only carry something like three billion people for an long period of time without irreversible damage to the natural order upon which we depend. And even then such a population would have to be thinly enough distributed to assure that people do not fall immediately to fighting over space and resources. In fact, for the natural world to heal the wounds inflicted by humans during the last century and a half or so, it would probably have to lie fallow for about five hundred years. The length of such a healing time is anyone's guess. Optimists would shorten it, pessimists would lengthen it.

There is a possibility, on the other hand, for the "developed" world to go into a long, steady (call it "natural") decline, leaving a mosaic of "cool" communities behind that in some ways resemble primitive cultures. Their "standard of living," as we like to call it, would be considerably lower than what we in the West are used to. It would resemble a melange of shanty-town societies, a version of what we now see in so many places known as the "Third World." Their quality of life might in some ways be superior to what we now see in those areas. But the thought of this possibility is generally repugnant to most of us.

Actually, of course, something like this "natural" decline did happen amidst the ruins of ancient Rome, ancient Egypt and in the Yucatan peninsula among the Maya. The ancient Mayan culture seems to have collapsed for a variety of reasons, among them population densities exceeding carrying capacity, with attendant wars, contesting aristocrats who spent enormous energy maintaining their royal and priestly castes, and the like. But the Mayan people are still there; so is their language. What disintegrated was an ideomass, an empire of ideas, beliefs and practices.

On the other hand it is possible to imagine a world with something like three billion people, organized and managed by highly sophisticated technological systems, advanced health care systems, splendid satellite weather prediction, wise agricultural ways, and forestry practices that could "go on forever." Such a world, its own kind of utopia, would be a sophisticated mosaic of cultures behaving in a reasonably benign way. Presumably, great tracts of social life would be sanctified and ritualized. It would represent a delicate balance between what is known rationally and what is appreciated, things known by the mind and things respected by the spirit. It would have to be wise enough in its ways not to destroy its own meta-rational undergirding. It would represent, hopefully, a new, liveable "Fourth World" pattern of cultures.

But there are several iron-laws that seem obvious enough to conclude that they will rule such a twenty-first century Fourth World. One says that scarcity and freedom are not compatible.

Everyone cannot have what they want and if what they want is increasingly constrained by what is available, the noose draws tighter. Further, there are two freedoms that are ruled by this law. One is the freedom to breed, which if exercised without restraint, makes things scarce. The other is the freedom to consume, which if exercised without restraint also makes things scarce.

And there appear to be but three ways to control the freedom to breed. One is some version or other of what Garrett Hardin calls "mutual coercion, mutually agreed upon." This option has a serious, if not fatal, flaw. Any population that refuses to accept such coercion, in a reasonably short time, would outnumber those that accept it. In other words, this option would likely go the way of chivalric warfare in medieval Japan when the gun was introduced. There is presently no way to assure that "mutually agreed upon" controls would remain "mutual."

The second means for controlling the freedom to breed could succeed, in principle. It is possible to forsee ruthless world-wide birth control on a scale not now imagined, not even in Peking. But given the fact that the world is splintered into hundreds of rickety nation-states, thousands of ethnic factions and uncounted tribes and localisms, it is hard to see how such controls could actually be enforced. On the contrary, one could anticipate intense resistance to birth-control dictates in many parts of the world, for religious as well as political reasons. One could even anticipate people taking their breeding habits, as it were, underground. Humans are, after all, animals, and the life force will remain powerful in the species.

The third possibility seems the most likely to occur. Even now, as we know, famine is spreading in ever wider areas of the planet. There are famines in a wide belt across Africa and apparently now in North Korea. And in recent centuries famines have scourged many parts of the world: India, Ireland, the Soviet Union, Somalia and China (both before and after communism).

Some argue that these famines were simply a consequence of economic stupidity or human political venality. There is merit to that argument. But since it is unlikely that humankind will simply forswear being stupid or venal, it is unlikely that these grim checks on population will disappear. In fact, the level of plain stupidity and venality can be expected to rise as the planet nears complete population saturation. The efforts by the Brazilian government or the Indonesian government to move their starving masses to new land carved from rain forest is an unhappy illustration of what I mean. These policies merely move the problem. At the same time they enlarge it. This is not to say that Brazilians or Indonesians are any more stupid or venal than the rest of us. Unfortunately it says that they are very like the rest of us, embarrassing as the thought may be to our favorite "weed species."

Such controls on population as famine can, of course, be called "natural."   That does not make them less brutal, unforgiving and painful to witness. And since death by diseases that are made worse by malnutrition, tuberculosis, malaria, AIDS and the like, plus all of the lethal viruses we are evidently driving out of their natural, biological lairs by deforestation, the area of the world that is famine ridden is far larger than we usually think it is. Pollution of fresh water supplies is also intensifying the impact of this deadly mix of controls on human numbers. The fact that the Rio Grande is now often called the Rio Sewer is not a mere coincidence, nor are problems in American cities with contaminated drinking water supplies.

The implications of all of this seem obvious enough. As scarcity increases, with food and fresh water in particular, rationing follows, determined by social class, caste, authoritarian dictate or simply the good fortune of being somewhere in a pocket of plenty. Unfortunately the freedom to eat when hungry and to drink clean water when thirsty are not inalienable rights. Biological reality has not arranged things that way.

To be sure there have been small steps toward a kind of limp application of Hardin's "mutually agreed upon" principles. The 1972 United Nations Conference on the Human Environment was one. So was the Rio de Janeiro Earth summit in 1992. Several multi-lateral treaties were signed in Rio. And there is talk now and then of GATT agreements becoming increasingly "green." But the vagaries of such agreements, not to mention the corruption that occurs in many member nations of international organizations, do not give us much encouragement.

Even if we grant for argument's sake that democracy and industrial privitization is winning out across the world, which writers such as Fukuyama claim, it would speed rather than slow resource depletion and environmental degradation. The collapse of the Soviet Union may momentarily slow collision with ecological reality in that part of the world, since inefficiency is sometimes on the side of Nature in our relations with it, it will probably make little difference in world-wide resource use or abuse. And "increasing the size of the world's economic pie," which is the way growth enthusiasts put it these days, merely underscores the seriousness of the problem. The planet has never been a pie and for all our gluttonous fantasies it is unlikely to turn into one. We will have to settle for a moon made of green cheese.

One may gain some insight perhaps, about the swirl and chaos of much of what is happening from the story, apocryphal to be sure, about Gustav Fechner, a learned German philosopher and the founder of psychophysics during the nineteenth century. Among other things, he came up with the principle of "just noticeable differences." The principal says that sensations come to us in a quanta and that stimulation must reach a threshold before a difference is noticed. According to one wag's account, a joke at the expense of the philosopher, Fechner sought to prove his principle by throwing a cat into a pot of cold water and raising the temperature so slowly that the cat did not notice when it had been boiled to death. Amusing, perhaps, but a story of some use here.

In cultures that change very slowly, as in Fox's "paleoterrific," there would have been little sense of change, unless some cataclysmic event occurred such as a volcanic eruption. As climate changed over thousands of years it is doubtful that people sensed that a great climatological process was in process. When the Sahara region began to dry up in prehistoric times, the people who left cliff paintings and effigy records behind them probably did not feel that enormous change was taking place.

This may or may not have been the case as well among the ancient Anasazi tribes of our own southwest. But there is evidence in this case that the shock of climate change was great enough to force people to leave their ancient homes suddenly. A Fechner effect might then have kicked in.

I believe this Fechner effect accounts, to some extent at any rate, for the fact that people who live affluent lives walled off from the tin-shack misery of the poorer masses by compounds with police at the gates, not only logically want to keep what they have, but bristle at the suggestion that they are in any real sense responsible for what goes on outside their compounds.

But since we are all one species and all inhabit the same shrinking planet, their isolation is illusory, maintained by the fact that they really do not experience "just noticeable differences," except perhaps for vacation periods when they visit pockets of poor people with quaint ways. Squalid back alleys and market places then take on a charm all their own, a "noticeable difference" to be captured on film, mounted in photo albums and circulated at cocktail parties back in the compound. If such people own a hefty bundle of investment stock they can then descant, over a tasty martini, why economic growth will "raise all boats."

Or, if it be a tasty second martini, with just a splash, and conversation shifts to "environmentalists" and the latest joke about spotted owls and snail darters, they may conclude that everything is just a matter of politics anyway, as they move solemnly toward the hors d'oeuvres table.

The boiled cat principle seems also to make a difference in the way different generations see things. The younger generation, which has not often had time to accumulate enough to appreciate what greed and financial self-defense can do for a person, will find the vigor with which old people try to protect what they have regardless of costs to society, curious. They may join enthusiastically in community groups lugging litter and old tires from the neighborhood stream and suspect that filthy water is perhaps not normal water. Oldsters in the town may reel off stories of great days of fly fishing on the stream only to follow the stories by suggesting that the reason why fish are floating on top of the stream instead of swimming in it is because "You can't stop progress." Which blurs the noticeable difference of things by spreading an old bromide across everything, including the sense of time. The point is that when change takes place fast, everyone notices. When it takes place slowly, few notice.

Costs, of course, always show up after the party. With scientific or technological achievements the same is true. In the beginning restraint loses out to enthusiasm. For instance, the costs of a clear-cut forested hillside do not show up at the time the trees are cut and the cash register rings. They show up when the rains come and mudslides follow and fish in the streams disappear. So it is with atomic energy plants. The bright lights they make possible are immediately obvious. The costs of disposing of radioactive waste does not show up for thirty years. So one may conclude that we, like the lungfish, live by Romer's Rule.

At the risk of repeating myself, I would note again that what Kuhn called "anomalies" are appearing all about us within the free-market paradigm that has dominated the Western world for so long. It not only includes heated debates over national debts, rising health costs, the ethics of keeping premature babies alive, or the aged alive as vegetables, as well as the epithet du jour about "environmentalists," it also shows up in all kinds of seemingly contradictory reactions within the science and technology community.

I might cite again the curiously contradictory quality of the so-called information revolution. It draws people together in an abstract way even as it distances them from each other in actuality. Fax machines, answering machines and call-waiting devices make physical contact increasingly obsolete. A conference call, however, is not really equivalent to warm hand shakes or hugs all around. So high-technology communication involves not just international telecommunications of the most impressive sort, it also accounts for lonely people with laptop computers pumping trivial information onto the information highway as they sit alone in coffee houses, hoping someone out there loves them. Hackers with genuine malice in their souls, of course, in a strange neurotic way hope the same thing.

As we try to imagine what the twenty-first century Fourth World might look like, it is important to remind ourselves that there is no such thing as moral progress. The pygmies of eastern Zaire, the Australian aborigines, or the Amazon Indians are as moral as any average citizen of the "developed" world. A visit to the ruins of Buchenwald or the crumbling remains of a Gulag labor camp, or a television broadcast of the latest massacre somewhere in the "modern" world ought to make that very obvious. And we should also remember that successful democracies such as ours or those of Europe have gone to war repeatedly and committed crimes that history has difficulty forgiving. So it is no time to be smug or self-righteous about what the future should look like.

All we know for sure is that the present time is full of portents, premonitions and unfinished trend lines on our graphs. What we may be witnessing now is a strange, new involutional phase of human domination of the planet, our species' grand ambitions turning in upon themselves. Perhaps this is what Munch's creature glimpsed and why he screamed.

Of course, the future cannot speak to us because it has yet to be given a tongue. Yet the clues to what it might say are strewn everywhere about our feet, like scribbled notes on scraps of parchment. Some of these clues contain ambiguous advice, like images left over from an unspent dream. Some are messages unwelcome to our imagination, like voices of a gaggle of uninvited, gossipy ghosts whispering to one another just far enough away so that we cannot make sense of what they say. Some of the notes at our feet contain raspy, vernacular truths that are homely and unkempt. And from a nearby hill-top may come the arrogant howl of some messiah with no credentials but voices in his head.

Aristotle reports that when Cratylus concluded that everything is changing he therefore also concluded that nothing could be affirmed. So Cratylus "finally did not think it right to say anything but only moved his finger."

Cratylus was wise perhaps, but surely tiresome too, sitting here, only moving a finger. But it is better to speculate than to be tiresome and that may be as good a reason as any to puzzle about the future.

Sources Cited

Adams, Brooks. *The Law of Civilization and Decay*. Alfred A. Knopf, New York, 1943.

Anderson, Christopher. "DOE and Texas Settle Superconducting Super Collider (SSC) Claims." *Science* 265 (1994).

Athanasiou, Tom. *Divided Planet: The Ecology of Rich and Poor*. Little, Brown, 1996.

Atlas, James. "Confessing for Voyeurs: The Age of the Literary Memoir is Now." *New York Times Magazine*, 12 May 1996, Sec. 6.

Attenborough, David. *The Private Life of Plants*. Princeton University Press, 1995.

Babbitt, Irving. *Rousseau and Romanticism* (first published in 1919). University of Texas press, Austin, 1947.

Becker, L. Carl. *The Heavenly City of the Eighteenth Century Philosophers*. Yale University Press, 1932.

Benditt, John. "Conduct in Science: The Culture of Credit. *Science* 268 (1995).

Bergson, Henry. *The Two Sources of Morality and Religion*. Doubleday Anchor, New York, 1956 (first published in 1932).

Bodley, John. *Victims of Progress*. Mayfield Publishing Company, Palo Alto, California, 1982.

Briner, Bob. *The Management Methods of Jesus*. Thomas Nelson Inc., 1996.

Brown, Lester R. et al. *State of the World*. Annual publications 1984-1996. Norton/Worldwatch Books, W. W. Norton & Co., New York.

Bruner, Jerome. "On Perceptual Readiness." *Psychological Review* 64(2), 1957.

Burke, James. *Connections*. Television documentary series, 1996.

Bury, J. B. *The Idea of Progress*. Macmillan, 1932.

Calhoun, John B. "Space and the Strategy of Life." *Ekistics*, 29(175), June, 1970.

Chandrasekhar, Subrahmanya. Quoted in *Newsweek*, 31 October 1983.

Chapin, F. Stuart. *Contemporary American Institutions.* Harper and Brothers, 1935.

Cohen, Joel E. *How Many People Can the Earth Support?* W. W. Norton & Co., New York, 1996.

Cole-Turner, Ronald. "Religion and Gene Patenting." *Science* 270, 6 October 1995.

Colin, Norman. *The God That Limps: Science and Technology in the Eighties.* W. W. Norton, 1982.

Daie, Jaleh. "The Activist Scientist." *Science*, 272, 24 May 1996.

Darwin, Francis (Ed.). *The Autobiography of Charles Darwin and Selected Letters.* Dover Publications, New York, 1958.

Dewey, John. *School and Society.* University of Chicago Press 1900.

Donoghue, Denis. *Walter Pater, Lover of Strange Souls.* Alfred A. Knopf, 1995.

Dyer, Gwynne. *War.* Crown Publishers, Inc., New York, 1985.

Easterbook, Gregg. *A Moment on the Earth.* Viking, New York, 1995.

Fesbach, Murray & Friendly, Alfred, Jr. *Ecocide in the USSR Health and Nature Under Siege.* Basic Books, New York 1992.

Feyerabend, Paul. *Against Method.* Atlantic Highlands Humanities Press. New Left Books, London, 1975.

Fox, Robin. *Consciousness Out of Context: Evolution, History Progress and the Post-Post-Industrial Society.* The Red Lamp of Incest: An Inquiry Into the Origins of Mind and Society. University of Notre Dame Press, 1983.

Frankel, Max. "Media Mongrels: Infomercials for Adult Degenerate into Kidpitch on the Web. *New York Time Magazine*, 2 June 1996.

Francione, Gary L. *Animals, Property and the Law.* Temple University Press, 1995.

Fukuyama, Francis. *The End of History and the Last Man* Avon Books, New York, 1992.

Furbank, P. N. *Diderot: A Critical Biography.* Alfred A Knopf, New York, 1992.

Gasset, Ortega y. *The Dehumanization of Art and Other Writings on Art and Culture.* Doubleday and Co., New York, 1956.

Graves, Michael. "A Case for Figurative Architecture: Buildings and Projects 1966-1981. Rizzoli, Reviewed in *Art News*, Summer 1983.

Hardin, Garrett. "The Tragedy of the Commons." *Science* 162, 13 December 1968.

Hawkings, Stephen W. *A Brief History of Time.* Bantam Books, New York, 1988.

Holden, Constance (Ed.). "Random Samples: The Last of the Cahokians." *Science* 272, 19 April 1996.

Holden, Constance. "Simon and Kahn Versus Global 2000, News and Comment." *Science*, 22 July 1983.

Honour, Hugh. *Burma: Splendor and Miseries.* The New York Review of Books, 13 July 1995.

Hough, Richard. *Captain James Cook, A Biography.* Norton, New York, 1995.

Huizinga, J. *In the Shadows of Tomorrow.* Norton, New York, 1936. Cited in *Science* 206, 16 November 1979.

Hulm, T. E. *Speculations.* Harcourt, Brace & Co., New York, 1924.

Hume, David. *Dialogues Concerning Natural Religion. The English Philosophers From Bacon to Mill.* The Modern Library, Random House, 1939.

Hunter, Mark & Crouch, Gregory. "Europe's Reborn Right." *New York Times Magazine*, 21 April 1996.

James, Bernard J. *The Death of Progress.* Alfred A. Knopf, New York, 1973.

James, Bernard J. "Human Behavior: some Biological and Cultural Determinants," in *Human Ecology*, edited by Frederick Sargent, II. ASP Biological & Medical press B.V. North-Holland Publishing Company, Amsterdam, 1974.

Jones, Laurie Beth. *Jesus C.E.O.* Hyperion, 1996.

Kahn, Herman et al. *The Next Two Hundred Years.* William Morrow and Co., Inc., New York, 1976.

Kaiser, Jocelyn (Ed.). "Random Samples: Stop Worrying and Love the Bomb." *Science* 269, 28 July 1995.

Kaplan, Robert D. *The Ends of the Earth: A Journey at the Dawn of the 21st Century.* Random House, New York, 1996.

Kennedy, Paul. *Preparing for the Twenty-First Century.* Harper Collins Publishers, Ltd., 1993.

Kennedy, Paul. *The Rise and Fall of the Great Powers.* Harper Collins Publishers, Ltd., 1988.

Klein, Joe. "The Unabomber and the Left." *Newsweek,* 22 April 1996.

Koestenbaum, Wayne. "Obscenity: A Celebration." *The New York Times Magazine,* 1995.

Koshland, Daniel E., Jr. "Animal rights and Animal Wrongs" (editorial). *Science* 243, 10 March 1989.

Kotre, John. *White Gloves: How We Create Ourselves Through Memory.* Free Press, 1995.

Kramer, Peter. *Listening to Prozac.* Penguin, USA, April, 1994.

Kroeber, A. L. *Configurations of Culture Growth.* University of California Press, Berkeley, 1944.

Kundera, Milan. *You're Not in Your Own House Here, My Dear Fellow.* New York Review of Books, 21 September 1995.

Kuhn, Thomas S. *The Structure of Scientific Revolutions* (2nd ed.). University of Chicago Press, 1970.

Laurence, William, quoted by Maurice M. Shapiro. *A Blinding Flash, Then a Foreboding. The New York Times Sunday,* 1995.

Leary, Warren E. "Gene Inserted in a Crop Plant quickly Spreads to Weeds, a Study Shows." *The New York Times,* 7 March 1996.

Lewin, Kurt. *Field Theory in Social Science.* Harper & Brothers, New York, 1951.

Linzey, Andrew. *Animal Theology.* University of Illinois Press, 1995.

Macadam, Barbara A. "A Conceptualist's Self-Conceptions: Joseph Kosuth." *Art News,* December, 1995.

Malthus, Thomas. *Essay on the Principle of Population.* Ward, Lock and Co., London, 1890 (first published in 1798).

Marinetti, Fillippo Tammaso. Quoted from *International News. Art News*, April, 1995.

Meadows, Donella H. & Dennis L. *The Limits to Growth.* University Books, New York, 1972.

Miller, Henry. *Tropic of Cancer.* Grove, New York, 1961.

Morton, Frederick. *Thunder at Twilight.* Charles Scribner & Sons, 1989.

Oelschlaeger, Max. *The Idea of Wilderness.* Yale University, 1991.

Pascal, Blaise. *Pensees.* Published posthumously in 1670. Washington Square Press edition, 1965.

Peirce, Charles S. *Chance, Love, and Logic.* Copyright 1923 by Harcourt, Brace & Co., Inc. Peter Smith, Publisher, 1949.

Perrin, Noel. *Giving Up the Gun.* Shambhala, Boulder, 1979.

Pollard, Sidney. *The Idea of Progress: History and Society.* Penguin Books, 1971.

Prunier, Gerard. *The Rwanda Crisis: History of a Genocide.* Columbia University Press, 1996.

Rappaport, Roy A. *Pigs for the Ancestors* (enlarged edition). Yale University Press, 1968.

Reif, Rita. "You Could Tell the 'Ism' by the Letterhead." *The New York Times*, 31 March 1996.

Romney, A. Kimball. *Predicting the Results of a Fee Listing Task from Cognitive Structure.* Presentation at the American Anthropological Association, Houston, 1 December 1977.

Rosenbaum, Ron. "Evil's Back: Staring Into the Heart of Darkness." *New York Times Magazine*, 4 June 1995.

Ryan, Alan. *John Dewey and the High Tide of American Liberalism.* W. W. Norton, 1995.

Schama, Simon. *Citizens.* Alfred A. Knopf, New York, 1989.

Schumacher, Ernst F. *Small is Beautiful: A Study of Economics as if People Mattered.* Harper & Row, New York, 1973.

Sharp, Lauriston. "Technological Innovation and Cultural Change: An Australian Case." In Hammond, Peter (Ed.), *Cultural and Social Anthropology: Selected Readings.* The Macmillan Company, New York, 1964.

Shenon, Philip. "The World: Energy-Hungry, Asia Embraces Nuclear Power. *The New York Times*, 23 April 1995.

Shepard, Paul & McKinley (Eds.). *The Subversive Science*. University of California, Berkeley, 1969.

Siena, Pisa & Hill towns (including Assisi). *Eremo Delle Carceri* (Prinson's Hermitage). Rome, tourist guide, 1996.

Smil, Vaclav. "Is There Enough Chinese Food?" A review of Brown, Lester R. *Who Will Feed China? Wake-up Call for a Small Planet*. Norton, 1996. Review in *The New York Review of Books*, 1 February 1996.

Smith, Roberta. "Still a Credo for Artists: Do as You Please: Performance Art is Reasserting Itself, Though the Body Misused is Likely to be a Mannequin or Made of Chocolate." *The New York Times*, 2 April 1995.

Soyinka, Wole. *The Open Sore of a Continent: A Personal Narrative of the Nigerian Crisis*. Oxford University Press, 1996.

Spengler, Oswald. *The Decline of the West*. Alfred A. Knopf, New York, 1926.

Taubes, Gary. News and Comment. "Is Science Lobbying an Oxymoron?" *Science* 269, 7 July 1995.

Taubes, Gary. News and Comment. "Plagiarism Suit Wins; Experts Hope It Won't Set a Trend." *Science* 268, 26 May 1995.

Taubes, Gary. "Gene Patenting: Scientists Attacked for 'Patenting' Pacific Tribe." *Science* 270, 17 November 1995.

Taubes, Gary. News and Comment. "Blowup at Yucca Mountain." *Science* 268, 30 June 1995.

Taubes, Gary (quoting Charles Fosberg). "Nuclear Waste Disposal." *Science* 271, 22 March 1996.

Tierney, John. "How to Get to Mars (And Make Millions)." *New York Times Magazine*, 26 May 1996.

Tuchman, Barbara W. *A Distant Mirror*. Ballantine, New York, 1978.

Unamuno, Miguel De. *The Tragic Sense of Life* (first published in English in 1921). Dover Publications, 1954.

Veblen, Thorstein. *The Higher Learning in America: A Memorandum on the Conduct of Universities by Business Men.* Academic Reprints, Stanford, California, 1954, first published by B. W. Huebsch, 1918.

Waldrop, M. Mitchell. "Neutrino Exploration of the Earth." *Science* 220, 10 June 1983.

Weber, Max. *The Protestant Ethic and the Spirit of Capitalism.* George Allen & Unwin Ltd., London, 1930.

Whitehead, Alfred North. *The Function of Reason.* Princeton University Press, 1929.

Wiener, Norberg. *Cybernetics.* MIT Press, Cambridge, Massachusetts, 1948.

Wilson, Edward O. *On Human Nature.* Harvard University Press, Cambridge, 1978.

Wittgenstein, Ludwig. *Tractatus Logico-Philosophicus.* Routledge & Kegan Paul, London, 1922.

Wright, Frank Lloyd. "The Concept and the Plan" (1928), in *Architectural Record, F. L. Wright, Writings and Buildings,* Edgar Kaufmann and Ben Raeburn, Eds. Meridian Books, New York, 1960.

Index